DO THE NEXT NEW THING

DO THE NEXT NEW THING

Pamela Lamp

Clovercroft Publishing

Published by Clovercroft Publishing, Franklin, Tennessee
www.clovercroftpublishing.com

Edited by Ann Tatlock

Cover and Interior Design by Suzanne Lawing

Printed in the United States of America

ISBN: 978-1-956370-33-1 (print)

For Mark
Here's to many more years of new things!

Contents

Section Four: GAIN NEW COURAGE

Section Five: DISCOVER NEW RELATIONSHIPS

Section Six: AND NOW WE WRAP UP

Section One

AND WE'RE OFF

FINDING MY *IT*

The bad news is that time flies.
The good news is that you're the pilot.
-MICHAEL ALTSHULER

Several years ago, when we still lived in Houston, a friend and I walked around the three-mile loop at Memorial Park. Sweating in the early morning heat and humidity, we caught up on kid stuff and the new Thai restaurant she'd tried on Saturday night and the book I couldn't wait to read. And then, as we rounded the corner of the gravelly trail, she dropped a bombshell.

"I wrote my obituary over the weekend," she announced.

"What?!" I stopped mid-stride and turned to face her.

She was close to 60 at the time and in good health. As far as I knew, she had no plans to leave this world anytime soon.

"It's one less thing for the kids to deal with when the time comes," she said.

After we finished walking and I was driving home, I thought about what my friend had said. *She wrote her obituary? Do people do that at my age?* Even though having a prewritten obit my sons could pull up on their laptops would check off a task for them, I didn't want to think about dying yet.

Besides, what would mine say?

I couldn't stop thinking about how my obituary might read while I showered and dried my hair. Like a song I've heard and can't stop hearing, I wrestled with its possible contents as I cut up carrots for dinner that evening, then tossed and turned in bed that night. I couldn't let it go.

The next morning, I sat down at the kitchen table and unfolded the newspaper. Sipping my coffee, I scanned the top news stories and checked the Astros' score. I glanced over the photos of fancy people at fancy parties and skimmed the real estate listings. And then I flipped to the obituaries.

The longer death announcements jumped out at me—the obits with several paragraphs detailing what the deceased had accomplished in their lives. The man who'd founded a heating and air-conditioning company and now left it for his sons to run. A woman who'd volunteered with the Red Cross for 65 years. Another woman served as a board member when the Girl Scouts voted to sell boxes of cookies door-to-door. Other departed individuals "wrote books, traveled the world, spoke to women's groups, inspired and cherished their grandchildren."

My final story—actually, my current story—puzzled me.

What did I want to do with the years I had left?

If you flipped through my calendar, my days were full. I headed off to workout classes three times a week and walked with a buddy almost every day. I gathered with friends for mahjong on Tuesday afternoons, Bible study Thursday mornings, and book club on the last Wednesday of the month. The occasional birthday lunch or neighborhood happy hour or volunteer session peppered my schedule. Most days, I was busy. And content.

Believe me, I was thankful every day for the life I had. I lived in a nice home with comfortable furniture and plenty of food on the table. I had happy sons, a great husband, wonderful friends, and good health.

But, in my mid-fifties, I wanted more. I longed to find something I was good at, something I was proud of, and do it.

But I didn't know what that something was. And I feared, at my age, I'd run out of time to find it.

What do YOU do?

As my boys grew older and moved on with their lives, the question caused the hairs on the back of my neck to stand on end. Every time an innocent person lobbed this question at me—across the table at a dinner party, at a meeting or church, or while making idle pre-takeoff chitchat in the adjacent airplane seat—I stammered and stuttered and froze. Dumbfounded, I'd shift my feet, eyes averted, looking for the answer to pop up in front of me.

It wasn't a trick question. It shouldn't be a tough one to answer.

But for me it was.

Nothing. I did nothing. Nothing that seemed accomplished or outstanding or produced income. My kids were grown and on their own. And I didn't have a job.

That was the honest answer, the one I wanted to blurt in response to that befuddling question tossed to me, again and again, over the last few years. After an awkward pause, I'd jokingly, apologetically, weakly respond that I took care of aging parents, visited kids in other cities, played a little golf, walked the dogs, and kept our house and everything in it in working order.

But I want more, I reminded myself after I'd maneuvered the conversation to a topic where my life wasn't center stage.

For 20 years, *What do you do?* was an easy question for me to answer. I was delighted—and fortunate—to stay home with our babies and help them grow into small children then bigger children then teenagers. I wore an array of hats I loved—chef, driver, cheerleader, nurse, referee, schoolteacher, social chairman, coach. And then one day "my job" was finished.

As my sons grew older and the years flew by, I knew I needed a plan. A blueprint for what to do when the kids left home and the house was empty and the days loomed long before me. This situation didn't sneak up on me. It wasn't a surprise.

But, like a pesky gnat or mosquito, I'd swatted the little voice away. The one whispering in my ear, urging me to figure out what I wanted to do once I had the time to do anything at all. I slapped the soundless chatter away without giving it the attention—I now know—it deserved.

Being a stay-at-home mom worked for our family—and for me. Before my older son arrived, I interviewed job applicants and taught employee workshops for a San Francisco bank. These were the days before Zoom interviews, the Internet, or even cell phones. I was a conscientious employee and, after I resigned, I came back every now and then to help out.

"Are you sure we can't talk you into returning?" my former boss always asked.

"Nope."

Yes, I gave up my career so my husband, Mark, could pursue his. But I liked being home with my boys. Back then, there was no such thing as online ordering or Amazon delivery or curbside pickup. If we needed milk or makeup or new sneakers, the three of us piled into the car and drove to the store. With no cell phones or email, I telephoned insurance companies and scheduled dentist appointments while my little guys played on the floor with Legos. My neighborhood babysitting co-op, with an organized system of debits and credits, was helpful. Moms swapped childcare for peaceful hair, doctor, or school appointments.

Like Michelle Obama, I was the "mom-in-chief."[1]

Over the years I tried a few enterprising projects from my home. Today, we might call them side hustles. There were a few years when I baked cookies in my kitchen and boxed up care packages for college students. For a while, parents paid me to assume the role of "nagging adult" and help their high school students organize and submit college applications. I proofread resumes for a company assisting displaced individuals.

None of these pursuits provided enough income to pay the mortgage, but I earned a little pocket money, controlled my schedule, and felt good about what I did. But … opening a bakery wasn't in the cards, and I couldn't envision correcting spelling and grammar errors for the rest of my days.

Since I couldn't imagine who would hire a 50-something woman who hadn't reported to an office for more than two decades, I figured I'd create my own job. A position I could take with me when I traveled with my husband or visited my in-laws or kids. I was smart and capable and knew I had something to contribute to this world before I left. I just had to find it.

My helpful husband had loads of suggestions for what I might do. Although his ideas sounded interesting to *him*, they didn't sound interesting to me. To add to my swirling tornado of emotions, I fretted *I* wasn't interesting. I was mired in quicksand.

I thought if I had a project and a purpose, I would fix myself.

Healthy living experts advise us to find a passion, a purpose. Studies show people who follow an activity that brings them joy and happiness live longer, more fulfilled lives[2]. Now that I'd raised my sons—and encouraged them to follow their hearts—I wanted to follow mine. I wanted to be more than I was right then. I wanted another *something* I couldn't quite put my finger on. But how did I pinpoint what I couldn't wait to get up in the morning and dive into?

Bob Goff, whose talks and books motivate people to accomplish their dreams and ambitions, suggests, "Know what you want, why you want it, and what you're going to do about it."[3] Sounds simple enough.

But how do you figure IT out? I worried about finding IT before it really *was* time to write my obituary.

GOODBYE HOUSTON

*In her experience, most endings turned out
to be beginnings in disguise.*
-CLARE POOLEY, IONA IVERSON'S RULES FOR COMMUTING

As I grappled with figuring out my IT and what direction my life would take, my husband accepted a new job. It was a good opportunity for him—for us—except for one tiny detail. This position was located 780 miles from our home. All our stuff—literally and figuratively—was in Houston, Texas. Twenty years' worth of friendships, history, security. A home with a basketball goal in the driveway, my kids' growth charts on the wall in the upstairs closet, and a garden full of tulips and caladiums.

Rather than uproot our lives, we decided Mark would commute. For a while anyway. He would do the test run, making certain the job and city were both good fits before we dismantled our lives in Houston and moved. We knew other couples who'd done this—successfully, it seemed.

Each Monday morning my husband kissed me goodbye, headed to the airport, and flew to his new office in Nashville. I stayed behind and plugged away with my commitments at home. When Mark returned on Friday nights, we'd spend the weekend catching up with friends and schedules and chores. Then it was time to start the cycle all over again.

We were trapped in a vicious circle.

And it wasn't working.

With schedules and work, the daytime hours were routine and "fine" for both of us. The nights were empty and long. We missed each other and grew tired of saying goodnight on the phone from beds hundreds of miles apart.

As unbelievable as it seems to me now, we lived like this for four years. As the months passed—quicker than one can imagine—we lived separate lives in different cities and traveled down parallel roads. Transactional communication, rather than meaningful conversation, became our norm.

We touched base on the details of our lives in an automatic and businesslike way. *Did you pay the insurance bill? Don't forget to send your mom a Mother's Day card. We need to order more air-conditioning filters. When is your flight due in?*

Finally, I reached out to someone. To help me fix things.

"What's going on?" the therapist asked.

"I've never had a problem I didn't think I could solve on my own." This was my first visit with a therapist.

She sat in the blue velvet chair, swinging her red suede heels ever so slightly, not saying a word. And so, I kept talking. I'd heard psychologists do that—remain silent so clients will fill up the awkward space. And I fell for the trick.

I rattled on about my lonely nights and my lack of a passion project and the separate existences my marriage had become. With a knowing, encouraging smile, she nodded. So I babbled on.

"I don't like this irritable, wound up, frustrated woman I've become. The one who compares herself to—and envies—those who seem to have it all together. She scares me. I need to make some changes. I need to find my IT. I need to fix myself. I need to fix my marriage."

After listening to me prattle on and on, she oh-so-calmly asked, "What's the first thing you want to change?"

The answer tumbled out of my mouth. "I'm not single, widowed, or divorced. I'm married. I love my husband. And I don't live with him."

"Can you change that?" she asked.

"Yes, I can." I nodded.

HELLO NASHVILLE

Nothing in life goes according to plan. Nothing.
And the sooner you accept that, the better off you'll be.
-Colleen Oakley, The Mostly True
Story of Tanner and Louise

And so we moved ...

Pulling my bathrobe tighter and grabbing my coffee mug, I stood at the window and watched the neighborhood waking up 13 floors below. Dogs meandered and sniffed on their first walks of the day. Armed with backpacks and cell phones and to-go cups, college students rushed to classes at the nearby campus. Songwriters, lugging guitar cases, made their way to studios along Music Row.

Packing cartons littered our living room floor. The final few boxes I'd shoved around for the last two weeks. Containers with labels indicating photographs and candlesticks and vases were crammed inside. I didn't know what to do with all that stuff. Where would it fit in our new apartment in our new city? I didn't know how it would be useful in this unfamiliar space. I wasn't sure where it belonged.

Just like me.

Starting over in an unknown town with unknown people was not the script I'd written for myself in my late fifties. I missed the comfort and security of my old routines and habits, those simple activities I didn't take the time to appreciate—until I left.

I craved the Mexican restaurant on the corner. The one where we'd gather after baseball games to down ice-cold margaritas, warm tortilla chips, and the creamy queso I could eat with a spoon. I missed running into girlfriends at the grocery store. Eating deep-fried Oreos in my cowboy boots and hat at the rodeo every March.

No one forced me to uproot my life and move away from everything I knew and loved. I chose this change—for us.

As I peered out the window, I cringed when I thought back to dinner with Mark last night. Like so much of our conversation of late, our meal together was a combination of two Pams. The brave me putting on my I've-got-it-all-together face and the scared me who took my uncertainty out on my well-meaning husband.

✜ ✜ ✜

While I waited for my fancy burger to arrive, I watched the servers with dangling earrings and intricate tattoos and beard nets scurry around us. I noticed the attractive young couples huddled at tables for two and the folks with dogs on the patio.

After taking a slow sip of his beer, Mark smiled and asked, "So … what did you do today?"

And that's all it took.

"I unpacked boxes and waited for the Internet guy all afternoon so our computers will work," I began.

But then …

"I don't DO anything," I continued in my petulant way. "I don't know anyone, and I miss my friends."

He didn't deserve that. That's not who I wanted to be.

✜ ✜ ✜

Pouring myself another cup of coffee, I glanced at a notepad on the kitchen counter. *Arrange Internet hook up, check. Connect television, check. Find a hairdresser. Look for a yoga studio. Register the car.*

Change bank account addresses. Schedule a mammogram. Buy stamps. Mail birthday card. Drop off dry cleaning.

I love lists. I like to have a plan. When I see all my tasks on paper, lined up in orderly rows, I am ready to face the day. With plenty of room in the margins for alternate options and scribbles, my lists give me direction. If I inventory all the assignments I hope to accomplish, anticipating what-ifs and pivot points, I tease myself into thinking I am in control. I am safe.

And I had no plan or list for this next chapter of my life.

Oh, I knew I'd find things to do—as listed above: Internet, dry cleaning, post office. But I wanted more than busy work. I craved a project to throw my heart and soul into. Sink my teeth into.

And now, since we'd moved, I had another problem. I had no friends.

Of course, I was happy my husband and I were living together again—all week long. But I couldn't slap down and dismiss my nagging thoughts. *How do I start over building a community? Find a purpose when I fear it may be too late? Be interesting to myself when I'm confused?*

✢ ✢ ✢

Several weeks earlier, as I packed for our long move, I cleared out the desk and bookshelves in our Houston home office. When I loaded papers and notebooks and files into packing boxes, I uncovered a handwritten chart I hadn't seen in decades. Examining the faded graph paper and pencil marks, I smiled when I remembered the night we mapped it out.

When we were newlyweds, more than 30 years ago, Mark and I sat down one evening with a glass of wine and put together a roadmap for our marriage. As young couples do, we imagined the various milestones we hoped to achieve in our life together—babies, jobs, better jobs, starter home, bigger home, remodels, travels, time for us—and the year these events would occur. Wow, we had our entire lives sketched out through the decades, line by neurotic line.

Some of those line items we plotted back in our twenties did play out according to our blueprint. Others, of course, did not. We chased careers and opportunities from Indiana to California to Texas and now Tennessee. Always before, jobs and kids were springboards to friends and relationships.

Packing up and moving to a new city at this stage in my life was not listed on that old paper I discovered. I had no strategy for making new friends and finding social groups here. I was uncertain how to reinvent myself and rebuild my life at this age.

For as long as I can remember, I've skimmed the last chapter of a book first. Then I don't have to worry about those characters I like and the predicaments they get into. I am prepared for the ending.

Too bad I couldn't do that with my own story.

Although I was frightened of what was around the corner, I knew I must—somehow—get a handle on myself and figure things out. Perhaps change might be good for a person at this point in her life. Maybe there are important lessons to learn from new beginnings.

I needed a plan.

DO THE NEXT NEW THING

You can't just be you. You have to double yourself. You have to read books on subjects you know nothing about. You have to travel to places you never thought of traveling. You have to meet every kind of person and endlessly stretch what you know.
-MARY WELLS LAWRENCE

Tossing and turning, I listened. Tap, tap, tap. It wasn't the door; it was an idea. Pushing its way into my head, into my subconsciousness.

This happens to me—a lot of times in the middle of the night. Or when I'm in the shower or cleaning the kitchen or walking. When I loosen my vicious grasp and stop racking my brain to remember the name of the movie or the restaurant or the person I ran into at the dentist's office, the answer comes to me. Or the solution to a problem I've mulled over for weeks becomes crystal clear in an instant.

"Do the next new thing," I heard in the wee hours of the morning.

Many years ago, I read *Finding Water: The Art of Perseverance*, the third book in a series by Julia Cameron, author of *The Artist's Way*. A friend had raved about the books and their methods to unblock your creative juices and steer you toward purpose and self-discovery.

"I must believe that if I just do the next right thing, a path will unfold for me," Cameron wrote.[4]

Do the next right thing.

After I read her book, Cameron's words came back to me again and again. They became my mantra when I was overwhelmed. Or didn't know where to start. They reminded me to concentrate on one step, not the entire staircase. Take one step, then the next, and the next. One action at a time.

When our sons were small, we moved from Northern California to Texas. My husband went on ahead of us, beginning his job assignment and searching for a temporary place for us to live. The boys and I stayed behind for a few weeks—handling the minutiae of a move to another state—before we boarded a plane to our new city.

I was excited for this next chapter in our lives but also drowning in the big picture and endless details. My priority was to ensure a smooth transition to this place for our four- and six-year-old boys. *Step by step, I can do this. Do the next right thing.*

With no apps or emails or texts back then, I spent my days on the phone. *We don't accept students midterm. I'm so sorry, we have room for one child but not both. Our waiting list begins at birth.* (Seriously, I heard that one.) *You missed our application deadline.* One tiny step at a time, I tracked down a preschool and a first-grade class and a place to park our puppy while we settled in. I prepared our California house to sell in a market that wasn't so good, arranged to ship our cars, and coordinated the packers and movers.

Just doing the next right thing kept me from going berserk—most days anyway—during that transition.

After moving to Nashville, I faced a different transition, a different city, a different stage in my life. And the lightbulb moment, in the middle of the night, was a variation on the mantra that worked for me all those years ago.

Do the next *new* thing.

What if I do one new thing, every single day for the next year, to acquaint myself with Nashville? I wasn't sure where I was headed or how this might help, but it was a first step, a move toward change.

At the kitchen table, surrounded by blank computer paper, my laptop, a pack of colorful markers, and a couple of free local magazines, I did what I do best. I made lists.

I'd like to find a yoga and a barre class. EXERCISE CLASSES, I wrote on the top of a page in bright orange marker. *I need a hairdresser, a dentist, an eye doctor, a car mechanic.* SERVICES went on the next sheet in blue. STORES TO EXPLORE, I printed in green marker. FIELD TRIPS in brown, page 4.

WALKS AND PARKS. PLACES TO VOLUNTEER. PERSONAL ACTIVITIES—like Bible study, book clubs, women's groups. PODCASTS AND WEBSITES. CONTACTS, page 9. Three friends in Houston had each given me the name of a woman they know here. I had three people on this list already! *I can bring my laptop to …* COFFEE SHOPS, page 10.

I attacked local websites and magazines highlighting "what to do this week in Nashville." I Googled and read and filled up my lists with simple, doable items. I wasn't interested in jumping out of airplanes or swimming in freezing waters. I brainstormed normal, everyday experiences. One thing led to another. One new thing led to another.

I needed light bulbs and batteries. Rather than press "Add to Cart" on Amazon, I read there was a hardware store in the cute neighborhood not far from our apartment. Added to STORES TO EXPLORE list, *check.* I learned yoga and Pilates studios and local gyms often allow you to try a class for free. EXERCISE CLASSES list, *check.* A woman my husband works with offered to help with doctor and hair recommendations. I added her name under CONTACTS.

I planned to stroll by the touristy spots downtown and walk over the pedestrian bridge, browse the local bookstores, pick up fresh tomatoes at the farmer's market, and subscribe to a few Nashville blogs and podcasts. Mark and I could check out the art museum, listen to live music in the park, attend services at the church on the hill. Or, I could go by myself. Where might I volunteer? Ooh, the nearby colleges offered all kinds of classes. I added CLASSES in pink. My lists got longer and longer, and I was energized as I filled them in with ideas.

I was excited. I was taking action to change my situation. I didn't know where I was going or what I was doing, but I liked the idea of a small daily step toward change. After making the bed, working out, and running errands, these lists gave me a goal for the day. They organized and cataloged my inner chaos and provided a regular contest with myself. I'd make meeting people and building community a game.

According to Gretchen Rubin and her book *The Four Tendencies*, I am an upholder. I'm the type of person who's likely to meet my inner and outer expectations. If I promise myself to exercise three days a week (inner expectation), I do it. If I commit to making those horrid solicitation calls for a parent auction, I do it (outer expectation). According to Ms. Rubin, upholders are disciplined and wake up each morning thinking, *What's on my schedule today?*[5] As boring as that sounds to many, that's me.

I like my ducks in a row.

I'll do the next new thing.

I tried my best to ignore the murmuring little voices clamoring to get my attention and burst my new thing bubble. *And how do you think this will help? Do you think you're going to meet a best friend in the produce section? You're going to do THAT alone? Hmmm, awfully indulgent. This list seems silly.* I batted them away—for the moment.

I've always liked assignments with colorful charts—and the chance to earn big glossy stars. In elementary school, I remember puppy stickers and heart stamps next to my name on the bulletin board chart because I read a library book. Or recited the week's spelling list without missing a letter. In my fifth-grade class, the chart for citizenship—probably called a kindness chart nowadays—was my favorite. Every time a classmate submitted your name because you helped them find a book or brushed them off after a fall on the playground or retrieved their lost mitten, Mrs. Hillier stuck a shiny gold star next to your name. I wanted those gold stars back then—and I wanted them now.

I plastered my lists all over our laundry room walls—my new thing for today habit tracker. I wanted to see my ideas, check off what I did, and chart my progress. I planned to add ideas to my lists as I learned of new things to do. Each evening, I imagined checking off an item and feeling accomplished for moving one step closer to this place feeling like home. And—hopefully—making new friends.

I was proud of my plan. Great job for "motion mode." But all this preparation wouldn't accomplish a thing unless I switched to "action mode." I still must execute and do the new thing each day.

Would I?

Both my sons, now in their twenties and launching careers in Washington, D.C. and Brooklyn, called later that afternoon.

"Happy birthday, Mom! What did you do today?"

"Well, I need an accountability partner," I said.

I could almost see their eyes roll when they looked at the photo I sent them of our new laundry room décor. But I wanted them to hold me accountable and ask me about my discoveries. And I knew they would. I've preached commitment to them for so long. Now it was their turn.

Oh, I was still wrestling with the idea of what my passion project would be. It should involve an income. Right? I continued to toss ideas around in my head and bounce them off my patient husband. But my project, for the next several todays, was to say yes to new things and get comfortable in my new place.

And so, I was off.

Day 1 of my Do the Next New Thing project. I walked to the office supply store on the college campus near my home.

"Will that be all for today?" the clerk asked, as she rang up my purchase.

"That's it." I stashed my shiny new packet of gold stars in my bag.

Later that evening, my husband took me to dinner at a quiet Italian restaurant I'd not been to. We toasted to 57 years—and my project.

The best gift I ever gave myself. A gift that would change my life.

Your Turn

Now, what about YOU?

Like the charts and notes plastering my laundry room wall, I invite you to make a list. Please don't worry about time or money or probability. Just jot down anything you might like to do in your town—and beyond. Or even in your home!

What sounds interesting or fun to you, despite its feasibility? My list didn't include skydiving or running a marathon or touring Egypt, but yours might. Your game, your rules. No item is too small or insignificant. This list is not all-inclusive. It's a jumping-off point to get you thinking—and dreaming.

Have you always imagined playing the cello? Would you love to paint the kitchen a new color? Check out the little boutique on the other side of town that you haven't made the time or effort to visit? Learn to edit photos? Decorate a cake with buttercream? Snowshoe? Knit a hat? Figure out how to find a podcast that interests you and listen to it? Get a library card?

Studies show by writing down an idea on paper, even if we never look at that paper again, we are more apt to remember it. The idea will take up residence in the back of our minds.

_____   _____

_____   _____

_____   _____

_____   _____

_____   _____

_____   _____

_____   _____

_____   _____

_____   _____

_____   _____

_____   _____

_____   _____

_____   _____

_____   _____

_____   _____

_____   _____

_____   _____

_____   _____

Section Two

APPRECIATE NEW WONDERS

MAKE WAY FOR SPECIAL

If I had my life to live over, I would have burned the pink candle—
sculpted like a rose—before it melted in storage.
-ERMA BOMBECK

On Day 3, I padded into the kitchen, opened the cupboard, and paused. Instead of automatically reaching for the black coffee mug emblazoned with THE MET or the holiday reindeer mug I used year-round, my eyes settled on the lone cup and saucer set. I hadn't noticed it in a good long while, and I'd certainly never, in the 25 years I'd owned it, sipped coffee or tea from it.

Before our move to Nashville, we sorted through our belongings and packed up our life in Houston. To prepare for passing our home of 20 years on to its lucky new family, we purged and donated and sold and consigned. I loaded the car with cartons of glasses and linens and books and cookware and schlepped them to thrift shops and charity drop offs.

Out went the dishes and linens and vases that looked worn and tired and out-of-date. I finally parted with the holiday decorations I shuffled around every season but never actually displayed. Goodbye to the necklaces and pans and bookends and platters I didn't really like.

But I saved—and transported to our new city—a few boxes stuffed with items I rarely used or wore. Because I liked them way too much.

Those items I saved for *special* …

The cream-colored silk blouse I rarely wore because it showed every speck of dirt—and had to go to the dry cleaner. The pretty soaps, lotions, and towels I'd received from girlfriends over the years? Those lived in the Houston powder room—the bathroom designated for guest use only. The delicate champagne flutes with the gold swirly etching appeared only when we had company. Too fragile for the dishwasher.

And my special cup and saucer from France.

Almost 30 years ago, I accompanied my husband on a business trip to Paris. We deposited our toddlers with my in-laws and took off on a journey to France—our first trip to Europe—without little people to dress and feed and bathe. I savored the cozy hotels with maid service, sidewalk cafes, chocolate croissants, and after-work window shopping along the Champs-Élysées.

In a lovely little garden-themed boutique, among the floral work aprons, dried lavender bouquets, and brimmed sun hats, I spotted a coffee cup and saucer. A twisting ribbon and bow, painted in the calmest shades of blue and green, wound their way around both pieces of the set. The dainty cup brought to mind a wicker chair on a sunny patio in the early morning sunshine. An imaginary—special—breakfast spot.

Bundled into my carry-on, that cup and saucer—and a little bit of Paris—traveled home with me. I placed my keepsake in our dining room cabinet, behind glass, on a shelf where it would be safe from little hands and accidental bumps.

And there it sat for decades.

When I did venture into the dining room, to dust or set the table with *special* china plates for a holiday meal, I noticed it. And somewhere, in the back corner of my mind, the cup reminded me of that wonderful trip and our one visit to Paris.

But it *never* crossed my mind to use it.

Until Day 3.

In our small living space, with limited shelves for decorative objects, I'd stowed my Paris cup and saucer in the kitchen cupboard. Alongside the dishwasher-safe, easily replaceable, so-what-if-they-break coffee mugs lined up and ready for morning coffee and afternoon tea.

The cup and saucer startled me when I saw it. Not in a frightening sort of way, of course. More of a *Hello, I didn't expect to see you here.* The same dainty set I'd looked at for years but didn't really see. Like the peeling paint behind the bathroom sink or the grease stain on the nightstand lampshade or the electrical panel that cried to have a piece of art hanging over it.

I *saw* it, but amid the day-to-day emails and chores and family worries, my mind didn't *register* it.

Until that morning—Day 3. Almost in slow motion, I picked up the cup and set it on the saucer. I smiled as I poured my coffee into that beautiful souvenir. And, leaning against the counter, watching the world from 13 stories high, my coffee never tasted so good.

Yes, the set should be hand washed, and it might break, and then there goes my treasure from that memorable trip all those years ago.

But it might not.

And drinking from that cup *was* special. Does this count as a new thing? Yes. Yes, it does.

Almost every day, I drink my coffee in that fragile cup. And plop it into the dishwasher. A bit of the Parisian blue paint has rubbed off, but that's okay.

In this new city in my new condo, I want a new start. And I want special.

GO IT ALONE

The deal is never anyone's fault. But you control the way you play.
-SHELBY VAN PELT, REMARKABLY BRIGHT CREATURES

Years ago, a Houston museum hosted a jewelry exhibit I wanted to see.
I reached out to a few friends to coordinate a field trip.

How is Tuesday afternoon? I emailed.

The responses rolled in.

Only if I'm home by 2.

I can go Tuesday if we go early.

I have a dentist appointment at 1:00.

Oh, wait a minute, that day won't work for me after all.

The planning and organizing grew so complicated—and exhaust-ing—that I gave up on the idea. We didn't go at all. The exhibit came and went, and I never purchased tickets. Because I didn't even consid-er going solo, I missed out on doing something I really wanted to do.

Many people go to movies, museums, restaurants, and other events *all by themselves.* It's not a big deal for them to set out on their own. They don't mind wandering alone, with no one to talk to. But, at that point in my life, that wasn't me. Going solo was out of my ordinary.

In my new city, there was a lot of unexplored territory to discover. Lots of new places to go and see. And, unless I wanted to sit home and wait until I found a friend or my husband was free to accompany me, I had to go it alone. So, I planned excursions for myself.

Over the next year or so, I covered a lot of ground. I added lots of gold stars to my charts.

✓ Popped into a violin shop

✓ Heard an Atlas Obscura speaker

✓ Visited a Civil War fortress

✓ Viewed holiday decorations at a massive hotel

✓ Strolled through a neighborhood to look at the architecture

✓ Took a free fly-fishing casting lesson at an outdoor store

✓ Saw a movie at a theater—by myself

✓ Signed up for a free photography mini-workshop

✓ Explored a zero-waste/package-free shop

✓ Visited a museum on a complimentary admission day

✓ Packed lunch and attended a free library concert

✓ Wandered through the local toy store

✓ Attended a mid-week church service

✓ Roamed the university art museum

✓ Meandered through an outdoor craft show

Julia Cameron, author of the Artist's Way book series, calls these solo expeditions "artist dates." Their purpose is to devote time to ourselves, by ourselves—"a festive solo undertaking to explore something that excites or interests us."[6] She suggests we pick something we'd like to do. Then do it.

Wandering the aisles of the toy store and the zero-waste/package-free shop wasn't hard. Attending the concert at the library and the photography workshop? Those activities were tougher. Perched on benches in the grand library courtyard, groups and pairs laughed and talked before the Beatles tribute band began playing. Not wanting to look around—and catch people looking back at all-alone Pam—I buried myself in my phone. My phone kept me company.

With practice, I got better at venturing out on my own. It was easier to show up solo the third, fourth, and fifth times. By the tenth time, I didn't even think of my lack of company. I let go of the fierce thought that I was traveling solo. My confidence gradually soared, and I began to look forward to hanging out with myself.

As an independent adventurer, I was intentional. I was focused. No, I didn't have a buddy to chat with about the latest TV show we were watching or where our kids might settle for their jobs. I had no one to confer with on directions and parking. But I also didn't have a companion to distract me from any part of the activity. I could absorb it all.

According to Dr. R. J. Jacobs, a Nashville psychologist and mystery author, I was a pursuer. "Happiness flows from the inside out. We must create the circumstances and then inhabit the space," he says. Rather than sitting back to see what might happen on a particular day, Dr. Jacobs says I "created an agenda, pursued, and felt good about myself in the process."[7]

My solo escapades, no matter how tiny, seemed interesting to me. I met friendly people to talk to, and I was learning Nashville. Instead of waiting for Saturday to roll around to take in a museum exhibit or stop off for a chocolate-dipped cone with my husband, I did those things on *my* schedule. I wasn't sitting around waiting for someone else to make me happy.

I made my own fun.

BABY STEPS

Enjoy the little things, for one day you may look back
and realize they were the big things.
-Robert Brault

When our boys were four and six, Murphy, a six-week-old golden retriever, joined our family. Each morning and afternoon, the boys and I headed out the back door, into our fenced backyard, with that rambunctious, adorable little bundle of fur. With baggies of tiny hot dog pieces, we'd coax her to sit, stay, walk on a leash, and come when we called her name. She'd do anything for those hot dog bites.

We didn't "work" with Murphy for a long time—perhaps 10 minutes each training session. But, after a while, our consistent, tiny steps paid off. Over the weeks, our pup's behavior changed. Murphy raced into the kitchen when I called her name. She'd lift her paw and shake on command. And, until one of the boys released her to eat from her dinner bowl, Murphy would sit and stay.

Organizing digital photographs into albums, digging through the mounds of paperwork I've shoved into a plastic bin at the back of a closet, and decluttering cupboards so my kids won't have to do it *someday* are tasks too overwhelming for me to tackle in one sitting. If

I wait until I have the time to attack the job all at once, that time will never come.

For me, it's easier—and more productive—to nibble away at a large chore in small chunks. I can almost always devote 10 minutes—most days—to the project. And then, at the end of the week, instead of the task rolling over to the next week's to-do list because I haven't found an hour or two (or 10) to devote to it, I'm surprised at my progress. However small it may be, I've made a dent. The paperwork stack is slightly shorter, I've cleaned out a whole cupboard, and I've sifted through a month's worth of photos. And this progress motivates me to set aside a few minutes the next day and the next.

Like with Murphy. At the end of each week (barring a skipped session every now and then), the boys and I trained our hot-dog-loving pup 20 minutes a day (two 10-minute sessions each day), seven days a week. Those minutes added up to more than two hours every week. In little snatches of time, Murphy turned into an obedient pup who was a joy to have in our home.

❖ ❖ ❖

On Day 29, I bought a fresh pineapple at the market, carted it home, and propped it on the kitchen counter. I studied it from all angles. Then I cut into it. I chopped off the leafy crown, peeled back the prickly skin, cored, and sliced it.

I felt a little silly counting that activity as the day's new thing.

But I did.

A great portion of my new things were small. And most didn't cost a dime.

✓ Signed up for a library card

✓ Parked in a different section of the Target lot

✓ Ate a persimmon

✓ Read a book on the balcony at night

✓ Packed a picnic and took it to the park

✓ Slathered my toast with ghee

✓ Unrolled my mat on the opposite end of the yoga room

✓ Ignored social media for the day

✓ Revived a rock-hard baguette

✓ Tuned into a podcast I'd read about

✓ Filled my tires with air

✓ Figured out earbuds

✓ Spiralized a sweet potato

Were these pursuits substantial enough to count as doing something new? Meaningful enough? Yes. Yes, they were.

Oh, switching my phone off all day or drinking my coffee with a splash of eggnog or calling someone I wouldn't typically call to wish her a happy birthday were not profound steps when viewed individually. Like watching my granddaughter grow, my laugh lines deepen, or my basil seeds sprout, the results didn't appear quickly and gobsmack me. They sneaked up on me. It was when I looked back at those teeny tiny new items, taken together as a whole, that I realized the effect they had on me.

Dr. Laurel Brown, a Nashville clinical psychologist, shared with me two documents that support the concept of big rewards from small activities—*Fun Activities Catalog* and *Possible Positive Activities*. Dr. Brown explained psychologists and therapists offer clients these—or similar—lists of suggested pleasurable activities as a standard treatment for anxiety. For individuals who may be depressed, unhappy, or experiencing a low mood, these simple, fun ideas are a great starting place to find enjoyment in life.

"It's sometimes difficult for people to understand the value in small, pleasant activities," Dr. Brown told me. "And tiny endeavors are not silly or hokey. There is real power in growing a plant, watching a sunrise, running through a sprinkler, drawing a cartoon, working a crossword puzzle, or singing around the house."

"The thinking," Dr. Brown continued, "is that one thing leads to another."[8]

These mood-boosting activities create a domino effect. If an individual finds the activity interesting or enjoyable, perhaps they might try another item on the list and then another. Little things lead to more little things. They add up to bigger things. Little things matter.

As insignificant as they seemed taken *individually*, my tiny new things did have an effect on my mood and behavior. I didn't sit or stay or come on demand. But I felt good about myself, went to bed happier, was eager to jump into my day, and wanted to learn *more* in my new town. And so, with a sense of satisfaction substituting as my hot dog treat, I continued to do the next new thing.

In my opinion, the little things set me up and prepared me to conquer the bigger stuff. Even if all I did was section a pineapple into bite-sized pieces.

PREPARE FOR SURPRISES

It is a gift in this life that we don't know what awaits us.
-ELIZABETH STROUT, LUCY BY THE SEA

On Day 5, I threw back the covers and sat up in bed, eager to get the day started.

While listening to the local news and scouring the newspaper, I picked up on a lot of excitement surrounding Marine Week. Every year, the Marine Corps visits a U.S. city to engage with folks in the community and raise awareness of the Marines and what they do.

Hundreds of Marines descend on the selected city with tanks and helicopters and boot camps and bands and wrestling teams. They set up exhibits, conduct demonstrations simulating military operations, and invite little kids to climb aboard the tanks and helicopters. And it's all free.

And that year, Nashville's Riverfront Park was home to Marine Week.

I tugged on my workout clothes and sneakers, grabbed my hat and sunglasses, and pulled up the destination on my phone. The sun was shining, the air felt crisp, and it was a beautiful September morning for my field trip.

With a spring in my step, I headed out on the 2 1/2-mile trek downtown. I followed the directions on my phone, winding my way through the historic Music Row neighborhood, the streets dotted with 1950s bungalows now housing record label companies and recording studios. Displayed on front lawns, banners announced songwriters' and music artists' number one hits.

I walked by then-empty (now high-rise-filled) lots and construction sites, with the bangs and clangs and beeps of bulldozers and dump trucks. I'd read about The Patterson House, a craft cocktail mecca with an unassuming street presence. *Note to self—return one evening for a drink with Mark.*

Past the apartment buildings and office towers and over the freeway overpass, I smiled at the tourists doing the same thing as me. Exploring.

Right, left, right, left. I meandered through the downtown streets, scattered with plastic beer cups and water bottles from last night's revelers. Country music blared from pedal taverns and party buses and honky-tonks. The smells of restaurants firing up barbecue smokers and chicken fryers mingled with stale beer.

I'd read about the iconic Ryman Auditorium and the Country Music Hall of Fame and the Frist Art Museum. All places—noted on my laundry room list—I planned to visit.

But I wasn't familiar with the old-timey candy store I stumbled into with bins and jars loaded with saltwater taffy and striped candy sticks and Necco Wafers. Or the record shop with vintage guitars and walls of vinyl records. Or the shopkeepers who designed sparkly stage costumes for country music stars and cowboy boots for presidents. I didn't know the musical history behind Tootsies, painted a splashy purple, until I ducked inside and looked at the walls lined with photographs.

A bunch of miniature surprises met me all along my route. Good surprises. I was a discoverer. And I liked that me.

I ended up at the military display, bordered by the Cumberland River and the burgeoning Nashville skyline. I wandered around the park, past military helicopters and kids climbing on tanks and brave young men and women dressed in uniforms and camouflage, proudly showing off their trucks and jeeps.

I didn't meet any potential friends here. Or discover a calling. But I did find a beautiful stretch of the city, some more places to explore, and some surprise and delight mixed in.

Without even thinking about it, when I was ready to head home, I automatically pulled up the directions on my phone. The same way I'd come, in reverse, I walked back to my apartment. I retraced the same streets and turns and intersections, passing now-familiar coffee shops and stores and hotels. Plodding by all the surprises that had, a few hours ago, delighted me. By clicking my route in reverse—the safe and familiar choice—I knew exactly what to expect. I didn't encounter any bad surprises on my way home. But I didn't discover any new ones—good surprises—either.

Thanks to the Internet, we can research whatever it is we want to buy, eat, wear, see, make, play, read, or do. With a few clicks, we can determine if the activity or purchase is worth our time. We can find out if it's safe, attractive, and will make us happy.

Before we step foot in a restaurant, we can peruse the entire menu online, complete with photos and reviews. Other diners will suggest which dishes to order and which to steer away from. We can discover the quickest driving route to any place we're going. A couple of clicks tell us which interchanges are bogged down by accidents or traffic. If desired, we can find out how a show or story ends before we turn on the TV or open the book. We see photos of a recipe before we dig in to cook it. When planning a vacation, we can look up the weather hour by hour, what the hotel room looks like, and even how gorgeous the sunsets or snow-covered mountaintops will appear.

According to Tania Luna, co-author of *Surprise: Embrace the Unpredictable and Engineer the Unexpected,* we "Google away delight."[9]

How often do surprises come along, even tiny ones?

In my case, how often did I *LET* myself experience surprises?

If I thought about it, I'd spent a decent amount of energy over-planning and overpreparing to ward off any bad surprises that *might* happen along. Like a general heading into combat, I mapped out a battle plan and equipped myself for all contingencies.

Need mosquito spray or wipes or sunscreen? Right here in my bag. Umbrella and extra sweater—check. Eat healthy meals, get enough sleep, lock the doors and windows, make sure no one follows you home, walk 10,000 steps, keep an eye on the car's fuel gauge.

But by working to eliminate the bad surprises, did I miss out on some of the good ones too? In this project, I discovered surprises sprinkled throughout my journey. And I wanted more of them in my life.

Your Turn

Do you have items in your home that you only use for special occasions—or have never used at all? Would you like to set a pretty table more often? Wear the red shoes that make you happy when you slide them on your feet? Light candles, buy peonies, wear the fancy bracelet?

_____   _____

_____   _____

_____   _____

_____   _____

_____   _____

_____   _____

_____   _____

_____   _____

_____   _____

Keep a running list of little things you might do. As you come across new ideas, add them.

Examples: Pour a splash of eggnog in your coffee, design a music playlist, organize your phone photos into albums or folders, make a video for your grandson who lives in another state, plant an herb garden, make snow ice cream, eat burrata.

_____ _____

_____ _____

_____ _____

_____ _____

_____ _____

_____ _____

_____ _____

_____ _____

_____ _____

Section Three

EXPLORE NEW SKILLS

PLAY IS FOR GROWN-UPS

*We don't stop playing because we grow old;
we grow old because we stop playing.*
-GEORGE BERNARD SHAW

The shop clerk stuffed bolts of fabric into their designated slots, lining them up on the shelves like colorful library books.

"Are you shopping for a special project?" she asked me.

"Oh, I don't sew," I replied. "But I love looking at all the pretty fabric."

"Well, don't you think it might be fun to learn?"

I stared at her like she'd sprouted antennae.

✦ ✦ ✦

On Day 123, I parked my car on a quiet side street and headed to the emerging neighborhood's busy main drag. I passed pricey, renovated bungalows with swings in the front yards, tricycles on the porches, and SUVs in the driveways.

Pony-tailed moms, juggling to-go coffee cups, pushed strollers with sleeping babies. Runners and walkers strode by. Residents waited patiently, scrolling their phones, while dogs drank from the water bowls set out by shop owners unlocking their front doors for the day.

I'd planned to explore this new—to me—section of town when traffic was light, and parking spaces were still easy to find.

Strolling down 12th Street, I discovered a boatload of surprises. Whimsical murals dressed up the brick walls of a barbecue joint, coffee shop, and Reese Witherspoon's clothing store. Tourists wearing cowboy boots, shorts, and glittering bachelorette sashes gathered bouquets from a flower truck. I made a mental note to return for a frozen treat at the paleta store.

Tucked between an ice cream parlor and a stylish boutique, a craft shop beckoned me inside with its quilts and cheery fabric in the window. I didn't sew and had no reason to buy fabric, but I'm a sucker for splashy, happy cottons.

As I poked around the tiny sewing shop, I imagined toddler dresses, baby quilts, or a summery top fashioned out of the yellow polka-dotted or sky blue striped or mint checked fabrics. I pictured a nursery, all coordinated and crisp in lavender elephants and muted gray swirls.

But ...

Do I think it would be fun to learn how to sew? Can it be fun if I don't do it well? Why would I bother?

✣ ✣ ✣

"We have classes," the shop clerk continued.

She had my attention. Classes mean people. People often turn into friends. I took the papers she handed me. To be polite.

"We have sewing machines to use here at the store," she said. "Just for fun. Come play with us."

Play? When was the last time I played?

I played a lot when my kids were young—played *with* them. We spent lazy afternoons at the swimming pool and the zoo. We collected lightning bugs and lizards in plastic jars. We rollerbladed, played H-O-R-S-E, and built Lego towers and trains. The dining room table was a wonderful mess of craft projects.

Then my sons got older. They played with friends and didn't need—or want—me to join in. More often, I served as the chauffeur, coordinator, and chaperone for their play. As they grew older still, I *watched* them play, from my spot in the bleachers, on baseball fields.

Did I even know what play looked like these days? Did I even know what I'd like to do for fun?

I signed up for a two-hour class. Even if I had no use for the lounge pants we'd sew, I'd be with people and maybe, just maybe, find a friend.

Day 145. Along with me, two 30-something women attended the class. The also-young instructor, a women's apparel designer in New York, guided us through the cutting, pinning, and assembly of draw-string-waisted shapeless pants while relaying stories about her single life in Manhattan. Although the four of us chatted while I wrestled with my heart-printed fabric—and played—I realized no budding friendships would come about. We chatted, but we didn't connect.

But a funny thing happened while I sewed and talked and listened and played. I didn't agonize about my lack of friends and how my life would ever come together in this new place. Not once did I worry about my family's health or my father-in-law's fall. As I battled those lounge pants, I forgot to fret.

Hungarian psychologist Mihaly Csikszentmihalyi calls this process "flow," and his research indicates this is one of the secrets to a happy life.[10] When we get involved in knitting, carpentry, or painting, the project gives us something else to focus on besides our problems. If our hands are busy with one thing, we can't worry about another. Our brains can't concentrate on two things at once.

I did *not* excel in that sewing class. But I did have fun. Despite my lackluster skills, I came home feeling good about myself. I showed up to the class, accomplished something, took the time to play, and enjoyed the time spent there. And I was proud of that me.

On Day 156, I returned to the fabric store.

I stacked three bolts of fabric on the counter, along with a pattern for an apron. I didn't need an apron, but I knew someone who'd love the cherries and stripes and cupcakes all sewn together in one happy combination. And I wanted to play.

At the back of our condo's hall closet, buried beneath luggage, a box of candles, and a Christmas tree stand, I pulled out the sewing machine I'd bought long ago. I hadn't turned it on in years, but it survived our move and the piles of donations and discards.

I studied the pattern's instructions and attacked my apron project. I sewed, ripped out mistakes, and chugged along.

And once again, as I played, I forgot to worry. I didn't think about the laundry sitting in the washing machine, what I'd fix for dinner, or what my next new thing would be.

I returned to the fabric shop every other day for the two weeks it took me to make that apron. "What do you need?" asked the same helpful clerk. She answered my questions and suggested tools to make the project easier.

And then, ta-da!

It came together. I had an apron with a pocket and ties and a daisy button on the yoke. If I looked closely, I saw all the imperfections. The crooked seams, pulled spots where the fabric got stuck in the presser foot, even tiny holes. But it was good enough.

I wrapped up that cheerful apron and shipped it to my mother-in-law for Mother's Day.

My father-in-law reported she got up each morning and tied the apron around her waist. She didn't plan to cook or clean. She wore it over her clothing and proclaimed to everyone she encountered in her memory care residence that her "wonderful daughter-in-law had made it for her."

Well, if Meme dressed in an apron every day, she needed more of a wardrobe. Once again, I returned to the fabric store and the smiling clerk.

"I need fabric," I said. "For more aprons."

She bagged up prints I knew my mother-in-law would love—pumpkins for the fall, holiday prints, puppies, bunnies, turtles, tea-cups, and penguins.

I cranked out a whole line of imperfect aprons for her. The second one was easier than the first. By the fifth, I was rolling.

For as long as I can remember, I shielded myself. I didn't try new activities where I feared I'd look silly or struggle or fail. Wallowing in uncomfortableness, I was like a human jack-in-the-box when con-sidering new experiences. Scrunched down into my tightly wound world, I was afraid to let go and spring into life.

What else did I miss because I didn't think I'd enjoy the experience? Or be good at it? What's the worst that could happen if I attempted a pottery or watercolor class or a jewelry-making workshop? Enrolled in an online language course? Gave pickleball a shot? Even when I turned out a misshapen pot (Day 66), a kindergarten-worthy painting (Day 45), or an inedible dinner, I tapped into another aspect of my world. I explored it, and it unlocked an urge to continue to do so.

Do I still sew? Besides the face masks I sewed during the pandemic with my piles of leftover fabric, I do not. But, nowadays, I do lots of playing.

More gold stars for ...

✓ Practiced scarf tying

✓ Took a free Internet class on calligraphy

✓ Rented a bike and rode on a trail

✓ Read a book all afternoon

✓ Attended a free concert at the park

✓ Picked strawberries at a farm

✓ Baked Nutella brownies—and gave them away

✓ Walked around a hotel and looked at holiday lights

✓ Packed a picnic and ate on a park bench

✓ Went to a bookstore author event

PULL OUT YOUR PHONE

Well, you learned something.
And any day a lesson's learned is a good day.
-MARIE BENEDICT AND VICTORIA CHRISTOPHER MURRAY,
THE FIRST LADIES

A couple of years ago, I spoke with Ruby, an 86-year-old New Englander and the go-to technology wizard in her retirement community. Her friends and neighbors turn to her when they're struggling with email or Internet shopping or signing up for an online class.

Ruby composed her church's newsletter until her mid-eighties, casts from the computer screen to her television, and is proficient with Zoom and FaceTime. The community members who say they don't need to know how to listen to podcasts, order from Amazon, and stream a movie frustrate her.

"Technology can be a bit daunting, but I'm not afraid of it," she said. Her tech skills offer her a lifeline to her far-reaching children and grandchildren and act as conversation starters with them too.

✦ ✦ ✦

Why can't technology fly in a holding pattern for a short while? I wish those tech geniuses—the ones who devise improvements and updates to the apps on my phone that work well *as is*—would give us time to catch up, take a breath, and press pause. Just when I congratulate myself for mastering the art of attaching balloons or confetti or fireworks to a birthday text, more newfangled tricks emerge. No matter how hard I try, I cannot keep up with technology.

I like to remind my boys that when I was growing up, our family—and every family I knew—owned a television set with four channels. We could access the three major networks and our local Indianapolis channel. After school, when I wanted to catch *Gilligan's Island*, I walked to the boxy beast, turned the on-off switch, flipped the channel dial, and waited for the set to warm up. With no recordings or Internet recaps, we watched our shows at the time advertised in the newspaper guide. If we missed our favorite show, we waited until the summer reruns rolled around.

If we allow it, technology can be the quickest route to feeling old. Many of us are no longer in the work world where shared documents and calendars, productivity logs, and meeting schedulers are the norm. Without young children, we might not need family organizers and babysitting payment apps and digital parental controls.

I get why some folks might argue that learning the latest technology tricks takes too much time or energy. Many resent the impact it has on society, where people constantly scroll phones in grocery lines, restaurants, and from behind the wheel of a car. Some fear security issues, while others choose to say hello to the familiar faces at the bank branch, post office, or hardware store. Or they simply no longer care to keep up with all that's available. It's easy to sigh and stop trying. I understand the sentiment "I know enough to get by."

It requires some know-how to watch a movie, listen to music, or transfer dollars from one bank account to another. And what about the touchscreen dashboards on today's newer cars? I fear my parents and in-laws, if they still drove, might sit in a freezing, silent car because they wouldn't be able to manage the techy climate and radio menus. For them, it's not intuitive, as my kids might say.

My phone and computer opened up an entire assortment of new things. On those days when I wasn't particularly motivated or didn't have a new thing idea, technology presented an endless supply of stay-at-home tricks and tips.

Since I like to make lists, I tried out the note-taking app I heard about on the morning news show. I researched photo editing apps and tried my hand at making the photographs I took look brighter and crisper. I put together a basic photo book, using images from a trip to Florida. The Internet overflows with step-by-step instructions and, once I learned to navigate YouTube, those videos provided help too.

Research shows we do not grow from taking an action we've always taken. Growth requires us to submerge ourselves into unfamiliar situations and tackle new—however small—challenges. When we send a text adorned with emojis or order our inaugural Uber ride or learn to read a picture book with a grandchild who is 500 miles away, our brain releases dopamine. We feel good, we want more of that happy feeling, and so we keep going. We plod through setting up a grocery delivery (Day 181), experiment with funny phone rings (Day 97), and practice French greetings with a language app (Day 80).[11]

During my project, technology new things became a domino effect. One new thing led to another and another and another.

Like music. I grew frustrated when I frequently didn't recognize the songs and artists nominated for the top music awards. When my younger, and much more hip, building neighbors told me which concert they were headed to, I pretended to know the band. "Oh, that will be great! Have fun!" Here I was, living in Music City, for goodness' sake, and I felt OUT OF TOUCH.

Like the shiny circular hot pink 45s record case I once toted to slumber parties, I wanted all my music and favorite songs (think '80s pop) organized in one, easy-to-play space. I also longed to discover music from trendy artists I didn't know—a bridge to a cooler, more in-the-know me. When I asked for help, assistance came in the form of a (much) younger person.

My niece, attending college in Nashville, guided me through a digital music service and its myriad of features. Need to relax? They have a playlist for that. Want to get pumped for a birthday party? They have you covered. There's even a button to press called Discover New Music. With her fingers flying over the keys at a lightning-quick pace, she showed me how to save music I liked, organize the songs into playlists, and create lists for every mood and situation.

And then she handed the phone to me.

My patient niece supervised as I muddled my way through what she'd just so clearly demonstrated. Unlike her, I was hesitant to punch the buttons and move songs around. *What happens if I make a mistake? What happens if all my data disappears?* "Don't worry about it," my niece said. "You can undo just about anything."

Like most her age who grew up with computers in their classrooms and phones in their book bags, she let go and experimented and waited to see what happened. She wasn't afraid to make a mistake and regroup.

Once I designed my first *(Happy Songs)* and then second *(Walking Songs)* and then third *(Songs for a Dinner Party)* playlist, the whoosh of accomplishment kicked in and motivated me to keep going.

The more I played around with my phone, the more I wanted to learn. Why was this important to me? It was one more way I felt interesting. Not sure I was more interesting, but I felt like it. And isn't that all that matters?

By the time this book is published, this list of phone hacks will no doubt be outdated. But then, I'll have more new stuff to try!

✓ Used Notes and Reminders

✓ Created an Instagram story (challenging!) and an Instagram reel (more challenging!)

✓ Recorded a YouTube video

✓ Set up—and paid for groceries with—Apple Pay

✓ Organized recipes into an app

✓ Installed Venmo for payments

✓ Connected the printer to my phone

✓ Monitored my workouts

✓ Discovered a white noise machine

✓ Practiced French

✓ Figured out how to use Zoom

✓ Scanned a document and signed it

✓ Read a restaurant menu via my phone

SWEET PERFECTION

*It's exhausting trying to be the person you think you want to be,
when all you really want is to be happy being the person you are.*
-SANDIE JONES, THE GUILT TRIP

The outfielders dropped fly balls, pitches soared over home plate, and the shortstop hurled a throw into the dugout. As we watched our beloved Astros play baseball, my husband stomped his feet and cursed at the television set. I howled.

"It's lots more fun to watch a sloppy game," I said. "Mistakes make things more interesting. Perfection is boring."

Did I just say that? Because it couldn't be further from my truth.

✛ ✛ ✛

I always envied my more devil-may-care, whatever-happens, relaxed friends. Those friends who make mistakes—and it doesn't bother them. The friends who *appreciate* the phone call from the dentist's office or hair salon. Otherwise, they may not remember their appointment. The women who mistakenly forget to return emails, texts, or phone calls. The trusting friends who actually *check* their luggage, not worrying that a baggage handler may accidentally send their bag on its own mistaken adventure.

I like order. Disorganization makes me restless, and mistakes make me anxious—or more anxious. I like to get things right—the first time. I've tried a lot of stuff once … embroidering a pillowcase, making sourdough bread, windsurfing, sculpting a buttery pie crust. And then I stopped. The results weren't good enough. I never gave myself the chance to improve.

One of my favorite things in life—along with books, the beach, and animals—are fancy sugar cookies in the shape of bunnies or shamrocks or pumpkins or pilgrims. Edible works of art with perfectly piped and luscious buttercream frosting. A Houston bakery, dangerously close to my house, offered these rich cookies with melt-in-your-mouth frosting. If they had a frequent cookie-eating club, I would be a premium member.

Like wallpapering a bedroom, altering a dress, or steam cleaning the carpet, I'd always believed cookie decorating falls into the category of *things best left to professionals.* But, on Day 215, I decided to give it a try. I assumed the endeavor would be difficult and fastidious, but I wanted to experience it. Once.

Because I held myself tightly in check and scoffed at doing something (potentially fun) that I wouldn't do right, I was certain the cookie decorating would be a one-and-done activity. *Would I ever tell my kids to give up after attempt number one?* Of course not! I'd tell them experimentation—and mistakes—are part of the fun of whatever it is they're doing for the first time. Lumps and bumps are how we learn and grow and figure out what we like to do.

As Upholders do, I prepared. I dug out my star-shaped cookie cutters, researched recipes, and scrolled social media for decorating ideas. At full throttle, the little voices blathered in my ear. *What a waste of time and money to make fattening cookies you shouldn't even eat! What a silly thing to do! These will not turn out well.*

But I turned my head and ignored those mumbles. I discovered an online cookie class, complete with video tutorials, recipes for the cookies and frosting, and two live sessions with the instructor.

"Remember to have fun, and don't be hard on yourself," the instructor said over Zoom. "Learning to decorate cookies will be a process."

She did not exaggerate.

As suggested, I spread out the tasks—and the monumental mess— over three or four days. I mixed the dough one morning, whipped up the buttercream frosting the next. Another afternoon I rolled out the dough, cut out a stack of star-shaped cookies, and baked them. Step by step. One thing at a time. Just do the next new thing.

And then, finally, I reached the decorating phase.

Have you ever watched cookie frosting videos? The mesmerizing ones that showcase a cookie decorator in a pretty white sweater who slides and glides the frosting onto a perfectly shaped cookie while a bracelet jangles daintily on her wrist? Trust me—it's not that easy.

There's a reason these little treats are $8 each in many bakeries. All sorts of things can go wrong. And, for me, they did.

It's a painstaking operation to color frosting just the right shade of holiday red (mine was more coral-colored), slather the concoction into pastry bags, and squeeze the globby mess onto a cookie. My kitchen was one huge MISTAKE. Runny frosting, thick frosting, pastry bag holes too large, pastry bag holes too small, pastry bags that burst at the seams, the soiled dishes, the sticky counter, the splattered floor, the mounds of dirty spatulas, bowls, and utensils.

"Chances are, your cookies will not turn out well on attempt number one," the instructor said. "It takes lots and lots of practice. But they will still be delicious."

And, for whatever reason, I listened to her. I wanted to improve. I wanted to allow my perfectionist self to enjoy the pastime and not worry about being good at it. After all, like we tell our kids, mistakes are part of the fun, and experimentation is the name of the game. And those sloppy lumps and messy bumps are how we learn and grow.

The second and third and fourth and fifth times I dragged out the mixer and rolling pin and cookie sheets, transforming my kitchen into a flour-spattered war zone, my skills improved. I learned some shortcuts and a system—and enjoyed creating edible art. I fell in love with this labor-intensive, sugar-loaded process that made my home smell cozy and warm.

In the last few years, I've practiced. I've baked and decorated loads of these cookies for family and friends. Most aren't close to perfect—the shapes are tough to decipher, the decorating lines are smudged, the colors aren't quite the right shades.

But every once in a great while, I get a cookie that turns out just right. A single Santa hat is baked with crisp, golden, sharp edges. The luscious buttercream frosting dyes to a bright and merry red. The icing consistency, my steady hand, and the pastry bag all cooperate to deliver furry-looking white detail flawlessly piped around the jolly holiday cap. I'm elated. The cookie is a home run.

And that's what keeps me firing up my mixer, donning my "messy clothes," and letting go of the outcome. Letting go of decorated sugar cookie perfection.

Just like in a baseball game, mistakes and imperfections are the norm. That's why a diving catch or a slam over the fence—or a cookie that doesn't glob or break or crack—is so darn exciting.

LET'S EAT

Nobody gets anywhere in life doing
what they already know how to do.
-Maggie Smith, Truth and Other Lies

For longer than I like to admit, I raced through the grocery aisles, grabbing pasta and chicken and broccoli to assemble meals based on a predictable rotating schedule. Although our family ate well, it was easier to prepare the meals I knew we liked, and my mental shopping list was neat and memorized. I was a kitchen robot.

Once the boys left home, when I could cook anything the two of us wanted to eat, the wind blew out of my sails. Dinner was fuel, a necessity, a chore I banged out at the end of the day. I threw dinner together without imagination or thought—chicken breast, vegetable, salad, done. I subscribed to a self-proclaimed adage, *I no longer must cook, therefore I don't like to cook.* After 20-some years, I'd grown tired of it.

One day at lunchtime, I leaned against the kitchen counter, eating store-bought chicken salad from a tub. As I scrolled through my phone, tapping hearts on Instagram feeds and pinning recipes to boards I'd never look at again, I stopped myself. Perhaps this project of mine had caused me to be more aware of what I was and was not doing. More mindful of what I did and didn't do. *Why am I admiring the photos of foods other people make?* I thought. *Why don't I give some of these recipes a try?* Do the next new thing—prepare a different recipe for dinner.

And so—on Day 135—cauliflower mashed potatoes became my next new thing.

Although fake veggie potatoes seemed like a trendy and healthy substitute for the starchy and carb-laden real deal, I had my doubts. Stirring chicken broth into the bland-looking pot of boiling cauliflower and then mashing it into a mushy consistency, I wondered how this concoction would be received at the dinner table that evening.

⁘ ⁘ ⁘

"What is this?" my husband asked, immediately noticing the interloper nestled among his chicken breast and salad.

"What do you think?" I asked after he took a mouthful.

"They're not bad. Are they mashed potatoes?"

"Sort of. And our culinary rut is about to change."

Based on the success of my pseudo mashed potatoes, I began to tackle recipes I'd previously labeled as *too much effort* or *not worth the trouble.* What's the worst that can happen? We may hate our meals and resort to cereal for dinner. For the record, we never did.

✓ Spatchcocked a chicken

✓ Baked—and ate—a pillowy pavlova

✓ Spiralized a zucchini

✓ Made sweet potato toast

✓ Experimented with kimchi

✓ Sauteed bok choy

✓ Prepared jammy eggs

✓ Brushed homemade harissa paste on chicken thighs

✓ Roasted chickpeas

✓ Discovered the lusciousness of burrata

✓ Wrestled with messy beets

✓ Tried a bibimbap dish

In my younger years, I loved studying foodie magazines and experimenting with all sorts of elaborate dishes. Then along came life and kids and schedules. I still flipped through those articles, but the recipes were for other people to make. People who had more time.

But, besides being a relatively easy way to check off my next new thing, I rediscovered my love of cooking which disappeared all those years ago. I now had the time to scour the grocery aisles for ghee and coconut aminos and chickpea pasta and persimmons. And figure out what to do with those ingredients.

In the book, *Lifting Depression: A Neuroscientist's Hands-On Approach to Activating Your Brain's Healing Power,* Dr. Kelly Lambert writes, "We get a deep sense of emotional satisfaction and well-being when we do something that requires some physical effort, including coordination and especially movement of the hands, and which also involves our problem solving and reasoning abilities."[12]

Cooking a meal, "poring over a scrapbook project, or knitting a sweater may distract you from the stress in your life and engage your brain in intense ways that are beneficial to your mental health."[13]

Although these healthy mashed potatoes were a minuscule new thing, my project seemed to have a domino effect. Stepping out of the usual cooking pattern seems small. But in my case—tiny steps, big rewards. The more new things I tried, the more I wanted to attempt. I felt a punch of satisfaction, a jolt of accomplishment. I felt up-to-date and informed, engaged and curious—and, once again, I liked that me.

It's also hard not to feel good when the house smells warm and cozy and sugary. Baking key lime bars and bourbon ball brownies and golden oat date squares made me happy. Giving these treats away to others—to our building employees and my husband's coworkers—made me even happier.

Of course, I don't make new recipes every day, and I've tried plenty I won't make again. I'm still cooking our old favorites and tried-and-true standbys. Don't let me fool you—I skip right over dishes with long lists of ingredients. And I am not about to run all over town looking for an unusual item I can't find at my regular grocery store.

Just as sticking to what dinners worked had become my standard operating mode, reaching out and experimenting and trying new recipes became a habit. And one I love. I still enjoy a good dinner out, and most Friday and Saturday nights, my kitchen is closed. But I am always thinking, *What can I make next?*

WIGGLY AND SOFT

When you go home today, ask yourself what you will change.
And then get started.
-Bonnie Garmus, Lessons in Chemistry

"Here, Mom, this is from both of us." On Day 106, my younger son plopped the square package, trimmed in a velvety red bow and shiny wrapping paper, in my lap.

Seated around the lighted tree, my sons took a break from sipping coffee and gobbling cinnamon rolls. As they exchanged conspiratorial glances, they waited for me to rip into the package. I sensed they'd done their gift due diligence and were pleased about this choice. And they hoped I'd be happy to receive whatever was hidden beneath that merry paper.

"Oh, wow!" I tore off the paper adorned with red-nosed reindeer. "Thank you so much!"

As I mustered enthusiasm and a tight smile, the words *work* and *mess* and *hard to clean* danced through my mind.

On that Christmas morning, I received a pasta-making machine. According to the package instructions, after I mixed (by hand) and kneaded (by hand) a basic dough, this stainless-steel device allowed me to hand crank that dough until it stretched into thin sheets of pasta. Then, I cut those sheets into strips to resemble fettuccini or spaghetti or lasagna.

It seemed like a process.

And, even on this festive holiday morning, my inner voices squawked.

Is this homemade stuff that much better? What's wrong with opening a box of noodles and dumping them into a kettle of boiling water? Yet another kitchen gadget to reside in my appliance graveyard cupboard?

STOP RIGHT THERE.

Those chirping murmurs mimicked the resigned, stagnant woman I was determined *not* to be. The woman who labeled activities as *too much trouble* or *not worth the effort*. The one who said *why bother?*

I refused to congeal.

Years ago, I listened to a sermon at a church service in Houston. I can't remember the specific religious details, but the main message stuck with me. *It's easy to live in a congealed state.*

According to the pastor at the pulpit, we all begin as fluid individuals. Like gelatin—when we first add water to the powder, and the mixture is runny—we flow and ooze around in our bowls of life. We are agreeable, adaptable creatures with curious dispositions.

And then, life happens. Like Jell-O settling on the refrigerator shelf, our circumstances cause us to solidify and stiffen. We become less willing to slosh around and experiment. If we're not open to new thoughts, people, books, and food, we turn rigid. We congeal.

After I unwrapped that pasta maker on Christmas morning, my family exchanged our remaining gifts, ate our sausage egg strata, and telephoned our long-distance relatives. We said our goodbyes, and the holiday ended for the year. As I packed away the chaos and decorations until the following December, I climbed on the step stool and tucked the pasta machine into the cupboard over the refrigerator.

And then I remembered the gifts Mark and I gave our parents in recent years.

Both sets of parents lived in the Midwest, with long, cold winter days spent indoors. The summer heat bothered them too. After they retired, all four complained of extra time on their hands and a lack of activities to keep them busy.

Each birthday, Mother's or Father's Day, and Christmas, my husband and I put our heads together to brainstorm ideas to help them alleviate boredom. My father, a former engineer, liked to tinker around the house. We gifted him a wooden duck decoy kit he could build, sand, and paint.

Mark's mom cooked every day. To make it easier to whip up soups for her church shut-in groups, we assumed she'd love the immersion blender she opened on Mother's Day. Or the mini food processor—to dice onions and carrots—we gave her.

After my mom remarked she'd like to try her hand at Spanish, we wrapped up some simple foreign language tapes. And, because the snow buried his backyard grill from November to April, we found a stovetop version for my father-in-law.

We were pretty darn proud of those gifts and couldn't wait for them to unpack their new toys and give them a whirl.

But they never did.

I know this because, when both sets of parents could no longer stay in their homes, Mark and I sorted through all their pictures, papers, dishes, and stuff accumulated over 50-plus years of living together. And we unearthed every single one of those objects in their original packaging.

It saddened us that our parents, quite mentally and physically capable when they received those gifts, chose not to try the items. I suppose my mother-in-law thought the new blending gadget wasn't necessary, Mark's dad considered the indoor grill "a hassle," and my mom decided she didn't need to know another language after all.

They were fine with things as is. Because, for the most part, that's how we humans operate. We're content to do what's comfortable and easy and routine. It's safer that way.

Because I did *not* want to congeal, I retrieved my new pasta contraption from its hiding place and plunked it where I wouldn't forget about it—front and center on the kitchen counter. No way, when the time came for *my* kids to sift through all my stuff, they would discover an unused pasta maker.

With lots of steps, ingredients, pans, and utensils, homemade lasagna is a big enough task to tackle without also making the noodles from scratch. Who does that? One Sunday, Day 135, that's precisely what I did.

And it was quite the endeavor.

Per the instruction manual, stirring the ingredients together with a wooden spoon is not the way to make lasagna noodles. Instead, following the indicated steps, I grabbed a handful of flour and created a "nest" on my quartz countertop. With sticky fingers, I gently swirled eggs and more flour into my nest and massaged the ingredients until they came together in a gummy sort of ball-like shape.

I was proud of my glob of dough.

Then kneading, lots and lots of kneading. Knead, knead, punch. Add flour. Knead, knead, punch. Add more flour.

While the dough rested, I set up my shiny new machine. After clamping it onto the kitchen counter and inserting the hand crank, I double-checked the instructions. After all ... *Don't want to do this wrong. Don't want to make a mistake.*

Throughout that lazy Sunday afternoon, I muddled my way through each step. I cut my dough ball into sections and fed those sections through the machine. Add flour, feed, crank, repeat. I cut my pasta sheets into lasagna-type noodles and draped them over a makeshift clothesline—wooden spoons supported by stacks of soup cans from the pantry.

I said it was a process.

Yes, making pasta from scratch was a flour-spattered production. But it was also satisfying, therapeutic, and fun. And almost relaxing.

I'll do this again, I thought as I scrubbed the sticky counters, swept the floor, and cleaned the tiny crevices of the machine. And I have. I've streamlined the process, and it's easier now.

Do I buy boxed pasta? Good gracious, yes! But it's not nearly as tasty.

When I announced my novelty project of trying one new thing every day, I worried what my kids and the women in their lives (both now my daughters-in-law) would think. I imagined their eye rolls, scoffs, and shaking heads. "Here she goes again. Another one of her ideas."

Like my short-lived resume-writing job, cookie-baking venture, or the charity project I outlined, I feared my kids would assume I'd abandon this project too.

But they didn't give up on me.

"What new stuff have you done this week?" they'd sometimes ask.

With that pasta-making contraption, they gifted me the ability to expand my world a teeny bit more. And another way to stay wiggly and soft.

Your Turn

If you had an entire afternoon with no other responsibilities, how might you play? Would you read around a pool—or swim laps in it? Bake a cherry pie, look through cookbooks, or research how to mix up a sourdough starter? You may enjoy wandering around a hobby or garden store, catching a movie, or watching a television documentary on Italy. Perhaps whiling a few hours away with a knitting, painting, or upholstery project intrigues you.

Again, don't consider feasibility or lack of time. And please don't say *I can't do THAT.* Or *I CAN'T do that.* Have you always pondered giving snowshoes a whirl? A ceramics class? Drawing cartoon animals with bright felt markers? Let's pretend you have the time, talent, and supplies to do whatever you want to do. What might that be?

_____   _____

_____   _____

_____   _____

_____   _____

_____   _____

_____   _____

Even if we think we've exhausted every activity our town offers, we haven't! All sorts of businesses and entrepreneurs provide free workshops and events. Grab the complimentary neighborhood leaflets and publications at the library (while you're at it, get a library card!) or the supermarket or a hotel lobby. Pour a glass of wine or brew a pot of coffee, go through these publications page by page, and make a note of any place, activity, or organization you might explore.

Read local blogs and newspapers for happenings around your area. (To find those blogs, search "blogs about things to do in Nashville," for example). Read about donut shops, craft fairs, bridge lessons, and walking trails. Wind your way through various articles; one website post will lead to another. Subscribe to the blogs or follow them on Instagram or Facebook. Say what you will about social media, but it is a great source for activities in your community and online.

_____   _____

_____   _____

_____   _____

_____   _____

_____   _____

_____   _____

Would you like to cook more appealing or healthier dinners for yourself? Make holiday treats for your neighbors? Find a muffin recipe to bake with a grandchild? Maybe you'd like to put the air fryer, instant pot, or mixer to use? Brainstorm ideas, recipes, and other ways to make this happen. (Examples: research cooking websites, spend some time browsing a kitchen store, pick a recipe and add the ingredients to your shopping list.)

_____   _____

_____   _____

_____   _____

_____   _____

_____   _____

_____   _____

Section Four

GAIN NEW COURAGE

FIND A GOOD BOOK

*In the absence of knowledge, the mind is an
amazing Tilt-A-Whirl of worst-case scenarios.*
- JODI PICOULT AND JENNIFER FINNEY BOYLAN, MAD HONEY

With limited numbers and a mix of personalities and dynamics, book clubs can often be hard to break into. A year before we left Houston, a friend—finally—invited me to join her book club. Once a month, I gathered with a dozen like-minded ladies for dessert, a little gossip, and a book discussion. Although I only attended six or seven meetings, that book club was one of the toughest things I left behind when we moved.

On Day 85, a sleeping shop dog greeted me as I pushed open the front door of Parnassus Books. An avid reader, I was eager to explore this—according to my research—Nashville treasure. Acclaimed novelist Ann Patchett and publishing industry veteran Karen Hayes opened this shop in 2011 after Nashville's only other independent bookstore closed.

And what a gem it was. Patting the shaggy pup as I maneuvered around him, I entered the booklover's tiny haven. Book-laden wooden shelves lined the walls highlighting book club suggestions, new releases, and staff reading picks. Polished oak tables held tidy stacks of books written by local authors. A whimsical children's section encouraged kids to read, play, and learn.

Like stumbling upon a beloved local bakery or a favorite coffee shop, I'd found my happy place.

"Can I help you find something?" A bookseller, uncrating a box of books, looked up.

I gushed that I was new to town, this was my first visit, and I loved the store.

"Well, welcome." She smiled. "Do you know about our author nights? We have them often, and they're very well attended. If there's someone you really want to see, come early."

"Oh, and we have book clubs," she added.

My ears perked up.

"I'm in charge of those," she said. "Come join us."

⁘ ⁘ ⁘

And so, on Day 118, I did.

I was nervous. Arriving solo doesn't seem like a big thing now, but back then, it was. I wasn't in the habit of not having another buddy to hang with when I arrived at an event. Typically, I at least had a connection to someone else—I'd seen them on the playground or a school meeting or a little league game—that enabled me to approach their circle and feel like I belonged.

The kind bookseller smiled as I chose a spot in the circle of folding chairs. As the 50 or so seats filled up, I observed the men and women of all ages and manner of dress, who came with partners or a friend. But many others arrived alone, and it was not a group where everyone seemed to know one another.

Shop dogs and customers milled about as the bookseller led the discussion. One attendee commented, "I can tell this is the author's first book. Her writing lagged a bit." Another woman brought up the confusing character arc. Another mentioned the plot's structure.

I loved the book, but I don't offer opinions in groups where I don't know people. What will people *think* when my comment is inarticulate, non-literary, and simple? What will they think when I'm *wrong*? But another woman, about my age and clad in workout gear, did speak up. She declared she "thoroughly enjoyed the story." That's it, that's all she said. Around the circle, I saw other heads bobbing in agreement.

After precisely one hour, the bookseller ended the meeting. We folded our chairs and stashed them in a corner. I patted the dogs in my path and sauntered out of the bookshop. I enjoyed this incognito group, and I was proud of myself for going—alone.

Maybe next time *I'll* speak up.

NUDIST FOR A DAY

Most women are haunted by the fear of missing. Of failing.
You must do the thing you think you cannot do.
-KATE QUINN, THE DIAMOND EYE

"Bonjour, madame. Isn't it a lovely day?"

Armed with a stack of plush towels, the beach attendant guided me across the sand, weaving among a smattering of sunbathers already settled on lounge chairs for the day. In my cover-up and sunglasses and floppy, wide-brimmed hat, I trotted after him, trying to keep my eyes fixed on his buttercup yellow shirt. Past the sun worshipers in various shapes, assorted sizes, and a range of ages. Men in skimpy neon briefs and women with their swim tops flung aside and breasts on display for all to see.

It was Day 274 …

And I'd finally made it to the South of France.

✤ ✤ ✤

Decades ago, my 20-year-old self conjured up a goal. A fantasy of sorts. I dreamed of, in the not-too-distant future, traveling to Europe, taking in the historic sites, and lounging—topless—on a beach in southern France.

At the time, that travel daydream smacked exotic. And starlet-like. I suppose I'd read enough racy romance novels to think reclining sans swimsuit top was unremarkable in that area of the world, on those beaches.

I pictured myself in a tiny bikini, all toned abs and legs, sun-kissed hair flowing in the sea breeze. Sprawled under a striped umbrella, bosoms to the sky, not a care in the world. And, of course, no kids in tow.

But first, I had to get halfway around the world to France.

And then I had to take off my shirt.

If I had the opportunity—someday—would I do it? Whip off the top half of a swimming suit, expose myself to the sun—and strangers—and lounge half naked for all to see?

What in the world would people think?

As a young mom, I cringed when the doorbell rang and a visitor dropped by unannounced. The caller was bound to notice the unfolded laundry piled on the table, utility bills and sticky notes scattered across the kitchen counter, Legos littering the floor. Not yet showered at 4 p.m., I hesitated to usher them into my beehive of a household. *What would they think?*

If my husband and I stepped out to another home for dinner, I panicked if I forgot the obligatory hostess gift—flowers, a candle, or a bottle of wine. After all, I was raised on the decree, "A good guest does not show up for dinner empty-handed." *What would people think?*

After our sons were off on their own, no longer requiring our supervision or money, my husband and I spent 10 glorious days exploring the French countryside. From Normandy to Brittany to Mont-Saint-Michel, we filled our days with Chablis and Camembert and croissants. We ended our dream vacation along the French Riviera.

So there I was, in the place of my long-ago daydream, on a stretch of beach overlooking the azure waters of the Mediterranean Sea. Pushing 60, long past toned and young and trim and svelte, I wasn't exactly the age I envisioned baring it all—or even some of it—on a public beach.

"Merci." The attendant adjusted my chair for ample shade, and I plopped into my chaise.

You need a new swimsuit, my well-traveled friend had advised me before I left home. *No one in Europe wears a one-piece suit.*

So now, I slid out of my cover-up and revealed a two-piece, skirted number, complete with a high waist and built-in tummy suppressors. Bravo for step one—revealing my swimsuit.

As I slathered on sunscreen, I surveyed the nearby beachgoers. I compared. Like mine, most bodies reclining near me—and not a swimsuit top in sight—had been reshaped by time, childbearing, and life. Big breasts, small breasts, saggy breasts, perky breasts, women with brown spots and wrinkles and cellulite. No one was staring (except me); no one cared.

Like mine, their bodies were far from perfect. And yet here they were, spending the day in a beautiful spot and doing what they wanted to do. They didn't care what anyone thought.

GET OVER YOURSELF.

No one was evaluating me—or my body. Throughout the years, I'd spent a fair amount of time fretting about what people might think of me or what I was doing. I'd imagined what my friend must think about my way-too-casual outfit or my son's tantrum or the grape juice stain on my living room couch. Guess what I now realize? People don't think about me nearly as much as I feared. They have their own pile of concerns.

And on that beach, halfway around the world, no one cared what my body looked like or that I was an exhibitionist for the day.

Like an amateur spy, I peeked over my sunglasses to see who was looking my way. Not a soul. Nonchalantly, I unhooked the clasp on my swimsuit top and flopped down on my stomach. And there I lay. Waiting for something to happen.

I was topless in the South of France.

I was one of *them*. I was doing it. I felt free and easy as the sun and breeze brushed parts of me they'd never touched before.

We all have blocks inside of us. Thoughts swirl in our heads, holding us back from trying and doing. *What will people think? I'm too old to do that. Who would hire me? I can't go there by myself. I shouldn't spend the money. I don't have the time. What if they say no? I will look so silly.*

When we remove these blocks, remove these *thinks*, we remove the reason why we can't and we begin to feel like we can. And that feeling keeps building. It gives us the courage to keep going and doing. It reenergizes us.

I got fully dressed to walk to the cafe for lunch. Mark and I sat beside a man I recognized from the beach. And another couple too. They'd seen me topless—they'd seen my breasts. They didn't care. No one cared but me.

When we returned to our chairs and umbrella, without missing a beat, I grabbed my book, unhooked my top, and broke free. Like anything else, it was easier the second time.

TRUST THE ODDS

*Believe me, if you want something different,
the only person holding you back is you.*
-Sarah Penner, The Lost Apothecary

Before I had a chance to overthink it—and that's a superpower of mine—I scrolled through the application on my laptop. *Name? Address? What shift do you prefer?* (Daytime, I'm sure it's safer.) *Why are you interested in a ride-along?*

I'd find it interesting to experience, firsthand, a day in the life of a police officer. My official response.

But the real answer—the one I *didn't* type in the box? I wanted to prove to myself I'm not as cautious and safe and anxious as I fear. As I know I am. I longed to put myself out there. Do something risky and brave.

I hit Submit.

❖ ❖ ❖

After several months of trying new things, I noticed I wasn't quite as hesitant to dip my toe into uncharted waters. Oh, I didn't leap straight off the high dive, but I didn't fret as much before I eased myself in. According to a therapist friend, the more we expose ourselves to anxiety-inducing experiences, the easier those types of activities become. Practice helps.

As I chugged along, day after day, new thing after new thing, putting one step in front of the other became a habit, just like the routine and monotony had become a habit. It no longer seemed as hard to stick my neck out and immerse myself in newness.

So. There I sat, in the police station at 6:00 a.m. on Day 357.

❖ ❖ ❖

A burly man rapped on the podium at the front of the windowless room. With piercing eyes and a no-nonsense expression, he called the workday to order.

"The team apprehended the murder suspect overnight. Great work. Today is business as usual."

As I sat—alone—at my table and looked around at the quiet and matter-of-fact police officers, I wondered which lucky man or woman drew the short straw. Who would I be riding with today?

The sergeant wrapped up his morning briefing, and the officers filed out of the room, on their way to squad cars and crime scenes and desk jobs.

"Meet Officer Allen," the sergeant said to me. "You'll be in good hands today. We hope you have a great experience. But remember, you don't have to spend the whole day in the car. Many people only ride for an hour or two. He'll bring you back anytime you want. Right back here. Just say the word."

As if I may be frightened ... And I was, a little. Jittery was a better description—like a hike in the woods with posted "Beware of Bears" signs or a bumpy airplane flight.

As an adult, I envied the folks who, at barbecues or dinner parties, assembled in groups and tried to outdo one another with their tales of adventure. Those devil-may-care souls who surrendered to the odds and let go. The bungee jumpers, gorilla stalkers, polar bear swimmers. Because that was not me.

Do I want to take a dip in ice-cold waters or clutch a rope and fling myself off a bridge? I do not. But I'd like to say *no, thank you* to the activity because I lack the interest or time or resources. Rather than because I'm scared.

I wanted to prove to myself I *could* handle a precarious undertaking. A supervised day with an armed and trained law enforcement officer in the seat beside me—an adventure with training wheels. I wanted to let go. I wanted to do this.

When we step outside our comfort zones—speak to a charity group, navigate a foreign airport, go on the first date after a messy divorce—we feel excited. And scared. Our energy levels rise, our adrenaline spikes. But we have a choice. Our fear can paralyze us, stopping us in our tracks. Or we can meet that debilitating fear head-on, stretching the possibilities in our life.

"Fear makes us feel alive," says Dr. Steve Orma, a clinical psychologist and specialist in the treatment of anxiety.[14] And I wanted to experience that feeling.

Officer Allen assured me that he and fellow officers in his precinct's detail actually *liked* having citizens ride along with them from time to time. A 16-year veteran of the Metro Nashville Police Department, he enjoys educating the public and showing people what life as a police officer involves. But without a bulletproof vest or Academy training, I am not certain I needed the "interesting and eye-opening experience" Officer Allen hoped to give me that day.

As we were buckling in and heading out, our first call of the day crackled over the car radio.

"MVA on highway, seems to be NIA, hook on way."

The officers do not patrol in pairs, so I rode shotgun as we responded to a minor crash on the highway. The next few hours "we" handled routine-to-him, fascinating-to-me "incidents," as they say in the police world. We pulled over a driver with expired tags. Checked in with a discount store about their rise in laundry detergent pod thefts, a form of currency in the drug world. Investigated a lead on a stolen pickup truck.

I trotted after Officer Allen with my mouth clamped shut and my eyes wide open.

And then, not long after a quick lunch at the courthouse, the radio squawked. In civilian speak—a domestic dispute between two men, next-door neighbors.

"I have to radio for backup on certain kinds of calls." He punched a code in the computer. "And this is one of those."

Officer Allen and a fellow officer strode toward the front door of the bungalow and motioned for me to follow. The nagging voices in my head chirped to a steady beat. *Is this smart to do? Is what I'm about to do safe?* But isn't risk and uncertainty what the day was all about?

I hopped out of the car, trusting Officer Allen to read the situation and keep me out of danger. The officers diffused the incident, taking one gentleman into custody, who rode with us to the booking station.

And that's where my "interesting and eye-opening" adventure ended, nine hours after it began.

"So, what did you think?" Officer Allen asked. "How was Day 357?"

On Day 357, in the police cruiser, I didn't get bogged down in all the what-ifs. Curiosity, excitement, and intrigue replaced my fear. I didn't worry about what might go wrong. I proved I can be brave and adventurous.

I trusted the odds.

And I craved more of that in my life.

KEEP ON WORRYING

My mom is fond of saying that if everyone threw their problems up in the air, people would race to catch their own.
-JAMIE DAY, THE BLOCK PARTY

As he leaned against the door of a New York City subway train, my adult son fainted. Like a giant redwood tree, he toppled over, his head crashing against the edge of a hard plastic seat. Out cold, he lay on the filthy floor, blood gushing from his eye.

A couple of good citizens called an ambulance, maneuvered him off the train, and waited with him until help arrived. He didn't fall onto the tracks—or worse—and called to relay his tale to me as he walked home from the emergency room.

"I'm okay, Mom," he said. "Don't worry."

Because he knows it's exactly what I do. If I worry about my husband's plane going down or my kids driving through a snowstorm or my mammogram results, I subconsciously believe the ruminating will fend off an actual disaster. By worrying, I feel in control. I have the mistaken notion that worrying prepares me and gives me a leg up on bad news. Nothing is going to catch me off guard!

But of the countless things I've worried about over the years, I had never worried about one of my sons fainting on a subway train.

One morning, I sipped coffee and skimmed a story in the newspaper. According to the article, writing down our worries helps to release matters from our minds. Getting those anxious thoughts on paper is freeing and gives us a clearer perspective on the situation.[15]

I am fortunate I don't have to worry about money for the mortgage, food on our table, or major health problems with my family. My worries are not significant compared to others around me. But the nagging thoughts swirling in my head and heart are still mine—and important to me.

And so, on Day 199, I made a worry list.

Per the article's instructions, I folded up my precious list and tucked it away until my designated worry time. At 4:15 p.m., I'd pull out my notebook paper and worry away for 15 minutes or so. Until then, I was not allowed to fuss about those burdens.

Could I make it through the day worry-free?

As the day went on—a meeting, a trip to the grocery store, yoga class—a few of my listed worries popped into my head. "Nope, not until 4:15," I said to myself. "Then I will deal with you."

At the appointed hour, I curled up on the couch, list in hand. *OK, here's what I'm anxious about. Let the worrying begin.*

But, as I looked over my checklist on the notebook paper, my worries seemed, employing logic and strategy … semi-manageable.

No matter how hard I ranted, raged, and chewed my nails, I couldn't solve the mass shooting problem in our country. My friend's cancer had returned, and I can be supportive. Unfortunately, there's nothing I can do to improve her health. Although heartbreaking to witness, it is impossible to reverse my mother-in-law's Alzheimer's diagnosis. So be it if my husband's flight is late tonight and we miss the party.

I crossed off those concerns I could do (relatively) nothing about. I let all this go.

And then I scratched off all those matters I get wound up about, which are none of my business. My son will have a girlfriend when the time is right. My husband can handle his skin check appointment without my instructions. More than once, I've offered my opinion about the lump my friend found on her dog's belly.

My worry list was growing shorter.

What remained were those final few items I could act on. Stuff I can control and is my business. I will finally call the doctor about my aching knee. I can check in with the friends I miss in Houston. And, as for the few pounds I've gained, I'll map out a plan to exercise more and eat less.

What did the worry list do? It caused me to focus on myself instead of focusing on and trying to control the lives of others.

Nowadays, when I'm overwhelmed, I grab my notebook and scratch out a list. I whittle down what I can and can't do anything about. And go from there.

Does this mean I am letting everything go? Heavens, no. But I'm learning.

My son, the subway fainter, traveled to our home for the holidays a week after his accident. On Christmas Eve, a doctor removed the stitches and noticed his cheekbone peeking through the roof of his mouth. But not to worry. He simply needed a little surgery.

APPLES, ORANGES, PEACHES, PEARS

But sometimes life presents opportunities at inopportune times.
And sometimes you have to ignore all the reasons to say no even if
there are a lot of them, and go with the reasons to say yes.
-SUSIE ORMAN SCHNALL, THE SUBWAY GIRLS

Hello, my name is Pam, and I'm a pear.

My upper body has always been—and always will be—smaller than my bottom half. It doesn't matter how many salads I eat or how many leg lifts I do, my proportions do not change. If I gain a pound or two after a weekend pizza and ice cream spree, I must suck in my stomach to zip up my jeans. If I cut out sugar and carbs for a few weeks, my tops get looser.

Some women are apples, holding their weight in the middle. A lucky bunch have hourglass shapes. Inverted triangles encompass larger-chested ladies with small hips. These slighter-thighed women are, of course, what I aspire to be because we're seldom happy with what we have.

According to an Internet search, I share my shape with Beyoncé, Kim Kardashian, Christina Aguilera, and Eva Longoria. But they have stylists who dress them, and I handle that task on my own. During my short stint as a clerk in a clothing store, I could not get over the women who came in shopping for an outfit to wear *that same night.* They'd pull on a pair of pants, and voila! No adjustments necessary. That never happens in my world. For as long as I can remember, for jeans to fit in the rear, I have to take a tuck in the waist. Although I am on the smallish side—some might describe me as tiny—I'm still a pear. A small pear.

Before my son's Brooklyn wedding, I made an appointment for a seamstress to alter my rehearsal dinner dress. Not surprisingly, the top portion of the dress was baggy. She took measurements, tailored the dress, and the rehearsal dinner was lovely.

A while later, the seamstress emailed me. She was developing a custom dress- and skirt-making business. On her new website, she planned to feature real-women models wearing her designs. If I agreed to appear on her website, she'd sew a custom skirt for me.

I didn't hesitate. Me, a model? I was flattered! *Of course,* I immediately responded.

She got back to me. *Great. Plan on two hours, here's the address, bring a white tank top and a neutral shade of heels.*

Well, I floated around our apartment for days. I was invited to model! Me! What a wonderful new thing for my list! Of all the church and volunteer fashion shows I'd attended over the years, I was not once asked to walk the runway.

The seamstress phoned the day before my big photo shoot to confirm I hadn't changed my mind.

Nope—I'm excited. And nervous.

"Please don't worry about your hair or makeup," she said. "Your head won't be in the shots."

Hmmmm …

In her perky voice, she continued. "You'll be our curvy model."

Excuse me?

"It's a body type." (I know what it is.) "Your bottom is bigger than your top." (I realize that.) "You're a Letter A. A pear."

She popped my proverbial red balloon with one giant dressmaking pin. In one quick jab, my excitement and pride and anticipation floated away. Replaced with embarrassment. She didn't choose me because of the beautiful way I'd show off her clothing. She chose me because I have a big ass.

Throughout this new things project, I enjoyed the fun of letting go—whether it be fear, perfection, worry, or what people think. It was liberating to lighten up, relax, and let myself live without all the constraints I'd kept locked in place for so long. But I also realized something else. I had to repeat the process of letting go almost every single day.

Yes, I am *less* worried, less hesitant, and less fearful, but I doubt those ingrained qualities will leave me altogether. Because, like my pear shape, that's who I am. I will never be the one who suggests scuba diving or sleeping under the stars or riding a donkey into the Grand Canyon. I may *entertain* those scary-to-me activities, but I'd have to have a quick chat with myself first. I'd remind myself to consider the teeny-tiny odds of a shark attacking my wetsuit, a snake slithering into my sleeping bag, or my mule plunging off the trail's edge. I will never be the one who jumps all in. I'll always have to evaluate and remind myself to let go. That's me.

The good I gleaned from this project lies in the fact that I can now release those constraints. Before, I deadbolted those in place and tossed away the key. Am I now fearless and worry-free? Ha! However, I seldom trap myself in a vicious loop of what-ifs and worst-case scenarios.

And so, after that phone call, I allowed myself a few minutes to pout about my curvy model status. And then—*Are we safe? Is anyone hurt? Am I healthy? Get over yourself.* Don't take yourself so seriously. Let. It. Go.

Day 333—photo shoot day. In the changing room, alongside a bevy of excited women pulling tank tops over their heads and slipping nude pumps onto their feet, I shimmied into the sleek red skirt the seamstress crafted especially for me.

"I am the curvy one," I said to the boyish-build model.

"I'm the apple," said another.

Another introduced herself as a yam. We had a banana in our bunch too.

One at a time, 12 women, embracing who we were and what we did and didn't have, turned to the side, to the back, the other side, the front, while the photographer clicked away. Because she wasn't shooting our faces, the photographer missed seeing our big smiles. But she didn't miss the claps and cheers as other models encouraged their fellow fruits. We weren't worried about being perfect or what people thought.

This is us. This is me. I am the fruit I am.

Your Turn

If you're interested in crafting a worry list, here's a place to begin. Please refer to *Keep on Worrying* for thoughts and suggestions.

_____   _____

_____   _____

_____   _____

_____   _____

_____   _____

_____   _____

ASK!

And this may be hard for you. It was for me. But it gets easier, I promise.

Wherever you go—local shops work best—ask about groups you might join or investigate. Ask at bookstores, clothing shops, running shoe stores, bike shops, community centers, libraries, coffee shops, senior citizen centers.

Keep asking. And make a note of the suggestions. If an idea doesn't appeal to you now, it may later.

_____   _____

_____   _____

_____   _____

_____   _____

_____   _____

_____   _____

Do you have far-reaching dreams of things you'd like to do? Someday ...

Items that seem silly to you—or unlikely—but they've lived in your innermost thoughts for a long time, scratching to work their way out and be noticed. *I'm here, I'm here, please listen to me,* they seem to say.

_____   _____

_____   _____

_____   _____

_____   _____

_____   _____

_____   _____

Section Five

DISCOVER NEW RELATIONSHIPS

DATING MY SPOUSE

*Is it possible that anxiety ends at the moment
when we no longer have time for it?*
-Ann Patchett, This is the Story of a Happy Marriage

A loooong time ago—before we had kids or a mortgage—I'd watch the older couples dining next to my husband and me in restaurants. Those folks who sat across the table from each other and ate their meals in silence. The ones I vowed we'd never be.

I'd nudge my husband. "We won't be like them. That won't happen to us."

Never say never.

✥ ✥ ✥

Years later in Houston, we celebrated our wedding anniversary with white tablecloths and soft music and a menu loaded with French dishes. And we floundered. The perfunctory conversation lasted through cocktails. We rattled off updates on obligatory topics—our sons and their girlfriends, necessary repairs to our 50-year-old home, work calendars, and elderly parent care. But then—after we gave our orders to the attentive waiter—we struggled.

How had we run out of things to talk about?

With our boys grown and gone, I suppose we both exhaled and took a rest from always being on—racing around at full speed between jobs and baseball games and grocery stores and parent meetings. We finally allowed ourselves to relax. Maybe too much so.

According to my confidantes—the girlfriends I met for coffee and wine and long walks—our quiet existence was not unusual.

"Marriage is hard. You can't expect the excitement to last forever," I heard over and over again.

Their assurances made me feel better. But I wanted more.

The therapist we visited in Nashville did not think we were falling apart. Still, I winced when she used words like *complacent* and *stale* and *stagnant* to describe our relationship. It seems we expected our marriage to hum along in a happy rhythm without a lot of effort or energy on our part.

I flinched when she compared our marriage to a withering plant. According to this wise woman seated across the desk from us, our relationship craved a good shot of nourishment and sunlight and fertilizer—tender loving care in the form of novelty.

Like humans are wired to do, my husband and I gravitated toward activities requiring us to stretch ourselves the least. We chose restaurants where reservations and parking spaces were easy to come by. We hung out with those friends we knew the best and were the most like us. Our date nights were predictable, safe, and routine.

"New shared experiences reenergize a relationship," she told us. "We need to be inventive, even with those closest to us. People have a need for adventure, and there's no adventure to drinks and dinner on repeat."

We were drowning in sameness.

As I tossed around what the therapist said, I realized that seeking out new things to do each day helped me. I was beginning to feel more interesting, less cautious, more alive. I wondered if the same principles might work for us. If I felt better about myself when I did new things, would shaking up our norm make my husband and me feel better about us?

My husband suggested our next date night activity. "You can do this. It's a good workout. I bet you'll want to do it again," he said.

I wasn't so sure.

On Day 182, as I stepped through the door of the rock-climbing gym, the smells of perspiration and wet sneakers smacked me in the face. Wiggling into the special harness and climbing shoes, butterflies fluttered in my stomach. I fumbled with the carabiners and belay equipment and rubbed chalk between my sweaty palms.

I was first-date nervous—the sort of emotion between excited and anxious. The same feeling I had when our relationship was fresh and emerging. Back when all we experienced was new and different.

Inching my way up the beginner wall—a vertical twister game, of sorts—I strained to reach the zigzag assortment of foot ledges and handholds. Time and time again, I slipped and lost my grip. Or my strength gave out. I pushed off from the wall with my feet, whooshed down to the base, and crept back up again.

Beside me, my husband wrestled his way up a more difficult wall. Together we grunted and struggled and smiled.

Still in workout clothes and baseball caps, we rehashed our evening's adventure over burgers and beers. We were proud of ourselves as a couple. We'd needed a kickstart, a homework assignment, to rediscover the joy of exploration and experimentation.

❖ ❖ ❖

Back to Dr. R. J. Jacobs, the Nashville psychologist and mystery author: "If a couple watches the same scary movie 100 times, it won't be scary anymore. If they hike the Red Trail three dozen times, been there, done that. It doesn't mean those activities aren't enjoyable. But they are used to them."

The same with relationships. We get used to things.

"The tendency in long-term relationships," says Dr. Jacobs, "is to favor the predictable over the unpredictable. Our brains are very good at justifying the old action, rather than doing something new."[16]

Novelty, we discovered, didn't have to be on a grand scale. Studies show novel experiences—no matter how small—reboot a tired relationship. Cooking new recipes together or sipping coffee in a trendy neighborhood or watching a wildlife documentary all contributed to our relationship's reboot. As newness became a habit, our spark—and conversation—returned. Besides arranging surprise dates, we:

✓ Walked after dinner—on a Tuesday

✓ Began a marriage journal

✓ Watched a Harry Potter movie together (neither of us read the books)

✓ Completed a couple of 5Ks (he ran/I walked)

✓ Taught him to play mahjong

✓ Played around with a Spanish language app together

✓ Cooked surprise dinners for each other

✓ Took photos of the neighborhood

✓ Read and discussed the same book

✓ Gave my husband flowers—he'd never received any

✓ Invented cocktails together

✓ Played new board games

Nowadays, we are the older couple in restaurants. We're the ones the younger diners may notice. But we are talking—most of the time anyway!

I NEED FRIENDS

I have the sense you're letting life happen to
you rather than figuring out what you want and
helping to make it happen—if you can.
-SALLY KOSLOW, THE REAL MRS. TOBIAS

More than a decade ago, I tried on dresses and frilly tops in the fitting room of a small clothing boutique. I wanted a new little number to wear to a special dinner the following week. For my 50th birthday.

I twisted and turned—admiring a black polka-dotted swirly dress—in front of the mirrored walls outside the fitting room. A spry gray-haired woman—I guessed her to be 82 or 83—popped out of her own changing cubicle.

"Honey, you look adorable in that dress," she said.

With her silver earrings bobbing, she smiled at her reflection in the mirror and the fuchsia linen dress she modeled.

"Oh, this will be perfect for *my* birthday party next week. How old will you be?" she asked me.

"Mine is a big one. I'll be 50." My voice lacked enthusiasm.

"Mine's a big one too. I'll be 100!"

Dumbfounded, I congratulated this woman and wished her a happy birthday. "What's your secret?" I asked.

She leaned her head close to mine and whispered in my ear. "Honey, I have a lot of friends. And I treasure them all."

Life *was* improving, I was making strides, and things *were* looking up. As I trudged along, day after day, new thing after new thing, I met a boatload of nice people. I lived my life, gained confidence, acclimated to my new city, and loosened my viselike grip on fear and hesitation. I got to know the curious person I wanted to be. But ... I still hadn't made *real friends*, and it was time to get busy.

Oh, I could trick myself into thinking I had friends.

For two hours every five weeks, while she cut and colored my hair, my hairdresser was my friend. Since she's a foodie, we compared recipes and cookbooks, and she steered me toward fun activities and restaurants around town. (The library puppet show is still on my list.) I exchanged pleasantries—*How was your weekend?*—with the folks I crossed paths with in our building. When I popped into the bookshop, a couple of the booksellers recognized me. At the Y, a few women and I would wave hello and smile at one another.

A+ for a good start. But I needed relationships. Real relationships.

We've all heard the science behind the benefits of friendships and sociability. According to Abraham Maslow and his famous hierarchy, the need to belong motivates human behavior. By belonging to a group, we feel we are a part of something bigger and more important than ourselves. Our need to belong drives us to seek stable, long-lasting relationships with other people.[17]

Friendships and groups motivate us to participate in social activities like clubs, sports teams, religious groups, and community organizations. Studies have found that people who feel a strong sense of belonging to social groups are much happier than those who do not. Research determined the more an individual identified with a particular group, the happier they were with their life. Friendships and socialization are important factors in longevity too.[18]

I was encountering friendly people, having some pleasant one-off conversations, and feeling good about all I was learning and doing. But I didn't have any friends.

By my calculation, I only required a couple of close pals. Those good friends you call at the last minute for a mind-clearing walk. The sort of friend you never run out of conversation with and know you won't come close to scratching the surface of topics to discuss. The friend you pound out texts to without regard to the time of day. "You won't BELIEVE what my mother-in-law did!" and "My son and his wife are pregnant!"

But, at my age, I worried it was too late to find those sorts of genuine friends. I feared I had run out of time to build up that kind of history. I craved bosom buddies, and I worried, at this stage of life, I would only find superficial companions.

Before I moved, three Houston friends each gave me the names and phone numbers (landlines, remember those?) of Nashville connections. The contacts were women they'd gone to school with or worked with at some point in their lives. The scrap of paper with the contact information on it resided—front and center—on my desk. Like a hairline crack in a window or a tiny rip in the bathroom wallpaper, I looked at that piece of paper and those names for so long I didn't even see the list anymore. My brain ignored it.

Without an email address, I had to pick up the phone and place a call to these women. And I thought about it—every day. But I always had an excuse. *It's too early. It's too late. They're preparing dinner at this hour. I don't have time to get into a long conversation now...* Looking back, I see that I feared they'd answer the phone. And so, I put it off. I avoided the situation.

I needed to up my game. I needed to up this Do the Next New Thing game. It's not hard to walk in a different park, listen to a new podcast show, or buy an ice cream flavor I haven't tried before. It's also less scary to say hello at a church meeting, spin class, or coffee shop community table and then shrink back into myself and my business like a turtle retreating into his shell.

I was an avoider. Extending a social invitation to someone I didn't know well—or at all—was hard, uncomfortable, frightening, and even somewhat odd. So I didn't do it. I avoided the encounter that caused the hairs on the back of my neck to stand at attention and my stomach to flip over. *What will they think? What if they turn me down?* It's hard to put yourself out there and risk their response.

But the opposite of avoidance is approach. And, realizing friends wouldn't materialize out of thin air, I knew what I needed to do.

And so I approached.

On Day 223, I forced myself to get up, get moving, and arrive at yoga a few minutes before class started. I approached the two women setting up mats around me. They were polite and friendly and welcomed me to Nashville. Then they continued with their conversation.

In my building elevator, I said hello and introduced myself to—approached—another rider with a dog. Pet owners seem less intimidating and usually welcome inquiries about their furry friends. I patted Cooper the Sheltie goodbye, and his owner bid me a nice evening as they hopped off on their floor.

But I persevered. I continued to be polite and curious and friendly. If I consistently approached people, I figured something good would come from my efforts.

And, one day, good stuff began to happen.

As I rolled out my mat in that same yoga class, one woman I'd spoken to smiled and headed my way.

"Do you have time to grab coffee after class?" she asked. "There's a place I like across the street."

I leaped at her offer. We drank coffee, exchanged contact info, and planned to meet for dinner the following week with two other women she thought I'd enjoy. The other two ladies didn't make it, but this wonderful, kindhearted, generous woman who helped me when I needed it most is, today, a dear friend.

Soon afterward, riding in my building's elevator, a soft-spoken, puppy-toting neighbor told me about a women's club associated with a nearby university. For $35 a year, the group offers classes, field trips, lectures, interest groups, and volunteer opportunities.

"Sign me up!" I said.

"I'll send you the info," she said. "And perhaps you'd like to join me for lunch next week."

Buoyed by the idea of *TWO* potential friends, I celebrated by picking up the phone and calling the three women on the list I'd shuffled around for so long. All they can do is say no, I thought as I asked each if they'd like to meet for a coffee. Turns out they all said yes.

Although I enjoyed our coffee shop conversations and bonded with them all, I sensed that two of the women had a lot going on in their busy lives. They had their own established female tribes and didn't seem to have the space or bandwidth to begin another friendship. I didn't hear from them again. Although disappointed, I understood. I'm sure I was that person before I was the newbie who needed other women to open up their lives and welcome me in.

With the third coffee meeting, I struck gold. Friend candidate number three was also at a point in her life where she needed new people and was seeking new friends, and we clicked. Today, we see each other often.

I've asked myself why I was hesitant to reach out. Why did it take so long to talk myself into finally making those phone calls? They were just phone calls.

Back to the blocks that we all have. Those blocks—our annoying thinks—that prevent us from diving into all sorts of pursuits. *Yikes, I won't be good at this. This looks way too hard. It will be easier to do it this way. What a lot of trouble. Let's just do it the way we've always done it. This will be a disaster. I can't do this.*

Tamping down, ignoring, rephrasing, or eliminating those blocks can lead to beautiful discoveries and enlightenment. If we give ourselves the chance.

Instead of embracing the negative, which our brains naturally move toward, we can retrain our minds to think of what might go right. *This might be fun. Maybe I can do that. It's worth a try. I can ask for help. I can reach out to her.*[19]

Making the friends I still have today, seven years after moving to Nashville, wasn't a quick process. But one tiny success was enough to motivate me to keep going, keep trying. To avoid staying stuck, we must be proactive. And, I promise, taking a deep breath and approaching gets easier with practice.

It was a big day when a woman I'd met at a bookshop group emailed me, asking me for a favor. "Will you meet with a friend of my sister's? Her husband accepted a job, and they've relocated to the area. She needs friends."

PRAYING TOGETHER

Ideas don't have to be complicated to be effective.
Sometimes simple strategies work best.
-R.J. Jacobs, And Then You Were Gone

On Day 200, I popped into a little gift-ish store—the sort of shop that sells candles and cheese spreaders and funny cocktail napkins. Browsing the book table, a title caught my eye. After I flipped through the paperback for several minutes, I thought, *Why not?* I headed to the checkout desk.

Couples Who Pray, written by husband-and-wife team Squire Rushnell and Louise DuArt, is a quick and easy read highlighting married couples, including several high-profile celebrities, who pray daily—*with one another.* Denzel and Pauletta Washington, Scott and Tracie Hamilton, Kathie Lee and the late Frank Gifford.

The book's message—and promise—grabbed my attention. It claimed praying together opens up a husband and wife to one another and creates a closer bond. In turn, this increases *intimacy* and *communication* in the relationship.[20]

I wrapped the book with a pretty ribbon, presented it to my husband, and braced myself for his reaction. This whopper of a new thing I proposed was most definitely not our style.

"What do you think? Shall we give this a try?" I asked.

The intimacy angle most likely intrigued my quiet-leaning husband, because I am certain he did *not* crave more conversation. We agreed to give the concept a shot. We had nothing to lose and, no matter their years together, what married couple couldn't use some help in the communication and intimacy departments?

I admit my expectations were low. Oh, I prayed, but I prayed silently and alone. With my morning coffee, before I fell asleep, driving in the car. The idea of asking for guidance with struggles and worries *out loud*? With my spouse *listening*? This prayer exercise may work for other people, but I doubted it would be successful for us.

The authors recommended a 40-day trial period. They predicted we'd see a change in our relationship and wish to continue. And so, on Day 207, our adventure began.

Like any Type A prayer partners, we outlined a strategy and established ground rules. We would pray in bed, after we closed our books and turned out the lights for the evening. Interrupting one another, comments, and side remarks were off-limits. Feedback and follow-up discussion must wait until the next day.

Praying in the dark—all snug in bed and ready for sleep—was my idea.

When my boys were young, they sometimes started a conversation as I tucked them into bed. They'd open up about their yucky school day, the mean kid who picked on them at recess, or a bad grade. I suppose the cozy blankets and the fact they assumed I couldn't see them made them loosen up. They felt more relaxed bringing up a difficult topic. I thought I'd feel safer—and less uncomfortable—with the lights out. Spilling my guts wouldn't be as scary.

And I was right.

With the room dark, mumbling my concerns and hopes aloud wasn't easy, but it wasn't as frightening as I imagined it might be. We didn't hold hands, gaze into each other's eyes, and use eloquent language. We took turns talking, then said amen and goodnight. Short and sweet.

At first, I prayed for our kids and elderly parents, safe travels, and friends who were struggling. I kept to nice, unembarrassing subject matter. Although my husband may think I'm a worrywart, I didn't want to open my mouth, unleash ALL my concerns, and remove all doubt. Although I'd been married to this man for more than 30 years, I was nervous to pray about the five pounds I'd gained or the dark mole I was convinced was bad news or the ugly blue lines on my leg.

But, as the nights progressed, I opened up, and so did he. With no distractions and nothing to do except listen, I realized my rock of a husband—who rarely asks for help—was worried about his lonely dad and the employee he had to fire. He heard I was restless and longed to explore and grow at this stage in my life. After all these years of marriage, we still had lots to learn about each other.

According to Dr. Hisla Bates, M.D., a pediatric and adult psychiatrist based in New York City, "Vulnerability is the ability to open up and take risks with your partner. With that vulnerability, there is growth and maturity in a relationship."[21] Our shared vulnerability—our praying together—generated a connection.

At the risk of sounding like a broken record, this new routine was easier the third night, the fifth, and the tenth. After two weeks, we were in a rhythm we loved, and our latest new thing became a habit. When Mark was traveling, we prayed together during our nightly telephone call.

If you had asked 50-year-old Pam if praying with my husband was something I would *ever* do, I would have shaken my head. Scoffed. "That's not us. That's not what we do."

Nowadays, we still pray together most nights. As the book I discovered in that gift shop promised, prayer did steer us toward better communication and triggered discussions. Physical intimacy? Hmmm—not sure about that one! I often wonder how this new thing might have affected our lives and family if we'd started this habit years ago. I'll never know. But it's another beautiful lesson—and reminder—for me. It's never too late to try something new.

NOT A WASTE OF TIME

But, Leah dear, if you have to preface something with "just be happy that," it means you're settling. And one should never settle.
-JAMIE BRENNER, BLUSH

During my first semester at Purdue, every Tuesday and Thursday morning, about 150 coeds and I crammed into a university lecture hall. Clad in a tweed skirt, tailored blazer, silky bow-tie blouse, and classic black pumps, Professor Janet Akers held court in the Intro to Fashion Retailing course. As we strolled into class, Dr. Akers examined our casual, preppy attire—cords, crew neck sweaters, penny or tassel loafers. She did not allow jeans in her classroom.

On one particular morning, a majority of students skipped her class. I can't remember if ice and snow blanketed the campus or students decided to jumpstart the holiday break or classmates had too much fun partying the evening before.

But I do remember Dr. Akers, peering up at the empty seats scattered among the tiered rows, was not pleased. She took the absence of so many students as a personal affront.

Preaching to the choir—those of us who *were* in attendance—Dr. Akers delivered a powerful lecture that day. In her clipped, rapid-fire New England voice, passion poured out of that woman. She didn't rage or scold or complain. She philosophized, shared life experiences, and relayed stories about her upbringing.

I've never forgotten her message.

Later, on those Saturday mornings when I did not want to roll out of bed, tug on a parka, and trudge through the snow to Comm class, I remembered her message. (And yes, Purdue held Saturday morning classes back then.) As a young career woman whose boss "requested" her to attend an after-hours compliance workshop, I thought of Dr. Akers and her message. Attending a middle school committee meeting, when all I wanted to do was tuck the kids into bed, pull on my pajamas, and curl up with a book, I heard her words. Even now, when I sit down to watch a TV show with Mark—one I'm not all that interested in—her message sings in my head.

I've never forgotten it.

"If you learn one thing at all—one tiny new piece of information—the activity is not a waste of your time."

Eager to meet people in my new town, I wondered if volunteering might be the golden ticket to friendships. But where to volunteer? Did I prefer a hospital, a museum, a food bank? I didn't know. I *did* know I wanted a flexible assignment, and I wanted to offer my help alongside other adults (and friend possibilities) who were volunteering at the same time. And, I needed to be busy. We've all been scheduled to chaperone a dance or a school carnival where we do little more than stand around. I wanted to work.

I pounded out a flurry of emails to museums, gardens, and the hospital down the street. For a variety of reasons, no leads.

The Country Music Hall of Fame and Museum, another Nashville treasure with a grand reputation, required a phone call to the volunteer coordinator. I explained who I was, that I was new to town, and I was anxious to get involved. The coordinator described the program, which seemed like an ideal fit for me. *Please sign me up.*

"We only do orientations twice a year," she said. The next training was several months away.

"Thanks. I'll keep trying." Like Eeyore, I hung up the phone and moped.

A week or so later, the coordinator called back.

"I have two other women who've contacted me, and I don't want to lose any of you. I'll do an extra orientation to get the three of you on board."

I snapped right back into Tigger mode. Visitors and locals flock to the Country Music Hall of Fame and Museum. Living in Nashville, I saw it as my civic duty to learn as much as possible about country music—and embrace it. What better place to do that than this museum?

To learn the ropes, my orientation trio toured the off-site historic RCA Studio B, the world-famous studio where Elvis Presley and other icons recorded their hits. We studied the Country Music Hall of Fame and Museum's walls of gold records, hallowed rotunda, and hours of operation. The recreated Taylor Swift tour bus, the Elvis Cadillac, the *Hee Haw* exhibit, and the entertainers' stunning costumes and keepsakes. A plethora of new things.

On my first afternoon of duty, I donned my jeans, white cotton shirt, and requisite black button-up vest emblazoned with the museum's emblem. Once I navigated the downtown streets overflowing with tourists, circled the parking garage a few times, and located the proper elevator in the massive museum, I reported to my assigned location. I was a greeter in the main lobby, smack-dab in the middle of all the action.

The museum boasted a huge roster of volunteers. Lots of people desired a community, wanted to get out and keep busy. Many, including husband and wife teams, were retired and enjoyed the social and mental stimulation. But younger folks craved the energy and opportunity too. Some sought a regular position at the museum and considered volunteering a stepping-stone to employment.

Alongside a volunteer partner, I greeted the throngs of people who filed into the museum. I explained the ticketing options, pointed them in the right direction, and answered the myriad of visitor questions. Did I know the answers? Ha! I had to stretch myself.

Where are the restrooms? Where should I begin my tour? How late are you open? I could handle those inquiries. Bill, the long-time museum employee and Nashville resident who staffed the main information desk, was my go-to for the tougher asks. *Where is the trolley stop? What's a good lunch spot? What might teenagers like to do in Nashville?*

Over the course of the volunteer afternoons, my responses became less canned, less robotic. Less uncomfortable. I adored offering suggestions and guidance to visitors from Switzerland and France and Canada. Joking with the college kids who popped in during their Spring Break. Chatting with the other volunteers.

I felt like a somebody.

Later in the year, I attended the annual banquet celebrating those of us who help the museum do what they do. Volunteers and our plus ones dined on a fancy meal and sipped wine in the rotunda lined with plaques honoring the legendary Hall of Fame members—artists like Sarah Cannon (better known as Minnie Pearl), Barbara Mandrell, Dolly Parton, Glen Campbell. Since we rarely worked with the same partner twice, very few of us *really* knew one another. But we talked and laughed and enjoyed the evening.

I didn't have to wear my vest.

My original goal—the reason I pursued the volunteer position—did not come to pass. I didn't make friends.

I made acquaintances. During my two-year tenure at the Hall of Fame, not once did I connect with another volunteer during my "off" hours. My volunteer partners and I "surface chatted" during lulls in the crowds and at the annual dinner, but we didn't socialize outside the office.

So, if volunteering didn't fulfill my mission of making new friends, was this stint at the Country Music Hall of Fame and Museum a waste of time? Definitely not.

With my volunteer position, I dressed, did my hair and make-up, and ventured out of my home. I had a job to do, an assignment.

During the two years, I took in all the permanent and rotating exhibits and learned a whole lot about my new city and its country music backbone. When Sandy, an avid reader, shared my shift, she introduced me to books by Barbara Kingsolver and Louise Penny. Randy, a much younger social worker, suggested bike paths, hiking trails, and under-the-radar coffee shops. Lizzie regaled me with tales of the music icon's grandson she dated.

Every day I volunteered, I added items and gold stars to the growing list tacked on my laundry room wall. I created a happiness loop. A more content Pam liked herself more, and that contentment transferred to my husband, family, and friends. My relationships improved, and I was more fun to be around. (Yes, I could tell.) Because my relationships improved, I was more content … And so the circle continued. Reflecting back now, I recognize that I'd stopped looking to others to make me happy. I grabbed the ball and ran with it.

When the volunteer coordinator retired, I stepped down too. After two years, I had settled into Nashville and found activities—and people—to fill my calendar. I tried and failed to track down Dr. Akers. Maybe I do not remember her name correctly, or she passed away before the Internet changed our lives. And other than the talk she gave on that day when I was 18 and most of the class skipped out, I don't remember much about that long-ago first-year class.

But I do remember I attended every one of her lectures.

Your Turn

If you'd like to meet people, how might you do so?

It took me a while to learn about the various resources open to people wanting to meet others. To save you time, here are some of the groups I discovered. Most of them operate in all areas, large and small. (I tested several geographic areas in Internet search engines.)

Newcomers groups – On your device, search *newcomers to Nashville* (for example) or *newcomer meetup Nashville.*

Women's or men's groups – Search *Lipscomb* (or college in your region) *women's/men's association/club/group.* When I test-searched this for various cities, the results showed business groups, philanthropy groups, and college groups not requiring graduation from that specific school to participate.

Lifelong learning groups – Try searching *lifelong learning* or *adult education.*

Alumni groups – Look up Panhellenic, college alumni, sorority/fraternity, high school alum groups.

Special interest groups – If you are active on Facebook, go to the Group tab. Within the Group section, search *walking group Nashville,* for example. You might also try other interests, perhaps *pickleball, food lovers,* or *photography.*

Church/synagogue groups – You don't have to be a member! Go into the religious organization's office, introduce yourself, and see what suggestions they might offer.

_____ _____

_____ _____

_____ _____

_____ _____

_____ _____

What new thing might you do with your spouse, partner, or friend? A date night to a surprise restaurant? Pizza and board games by the fire? Charades? Cook paella together? Walk a 5K at holiday time?

_____ _____

_____ _____

_____ _____

_____ _____

_____ _____

Are you interested in volunteering? What sorts of projects might interest you? For opportunities in your area, search *volunteer Huntington Indiana,* for example.

——————————————— ———————————————

——————————————— ———————————————

——————————————— ———————————————

——————————————— ———————————————

——————————————— ———————————————

——————————————— ———————————————

Section Six

AND NOW WE WRAP UP

THE DOMINO EFFECT

You can't go back and change the beginning,
but you can start where you are and change the ending.
-C. S. Lewis

When I joined my husband in Nashville, I moved into the condominium unit he'd rented for his commuting work weeks. The 1,000-square-foot apartment consisted of *one* bedroom, *one* bathroom with a single counter and sink, and *one* closet for clothing, shoes, and coats. The unit was efficient and airy and modern and perfect for one person. For two people, the space was tight.

We'd kept—and transported to Nashville—only what we loved, needed, and used. A la Marie Kondo, if an item didn't "spark joy," it didn't make the trip. With our cramped quarters, we learned to be discriminating about the belongings surrounding us. During the two years we lived in that unit, not once did we say, *I wish we still had this,* or *We shouldn't have gotten rid of that.* For us, getting rid of stuff was liberating.

And then, a larger place I had my eye on came up for sale. We bought it. Same building, but with an extra bedroom, another bath, bigger rooms, additional closets. More space for my husband to set up an office, me to cook and bake, and family to stay.

More space for us to spread out.

After we unpacked and tucked all our possessions into their new resting spots, a friend stopped by for dinner. Touring her through our new home, I flung doors open for her to look—and marvel. *See the cupboard over the fridge?* Empty! Note the top shelves of the kitchen cabinets. The drawers in the second bedroom. The additional walk-in closet with hanging racks and shelves. Empty! Empty! Empty!

The domino effect was a slow one. I didn't realize what was happening until, a couple of years later, I opened a drawer bulging at the seams. *Here we go again.* A collection of *stuff* chain reaction.

Since moving into the larger place, I had no reason to be ruthless and selective or ask myself if I *needed* the item. I saved every fabric shopping bag from a store or promotional giveaway. In case I had to ship a gift, I stockpiled an assortment of cardboard Amazon boxes. Instead of immediately passing on to a friend the latest book I read, I stashed it on a shelf. When I bought new sheets, sneakers, or a saucepan, I saved the older version. As a spare.

I had the space. And so I filled it up.

My neighbor once told me that her (rather extensive) remodeling project began with touching up the paint scratches in her bedroom. As she feathered in the fresh blue paint on the dark scuff marks, she decided she might like to have gray walls instead. After she had gray walls, the rug didn't match. Then the draperies didn't look quite right. The headboard seemed dated. And the domino effect continued ...

The farm stands around Nashville are some of my favorite things about living here. Each April, wooden tables and white awnings pop up in parking lots around town. Soon, farmers deliver their daily bounty, freshly picked and warm from the summer sunshine.

On Day 242, on my way home from an exercise class at the Y, I stopped at one of these produce stands. I piled my strawberries, green beans, cucumbers, and tomatoes—oh, those heirloom tomatoes— on the makeshift counter for the attendant to weigh, price, and bag.

Although Venmo (Day 67) and credit cards are accepted now, they weren't back then. And I had no cash.

The clerk smiled. "Oh, just catch up with us next time."

Over the summer, I dropped by several more of those produce stands scattered around the city. One afternoon (Day 260), another shopper—lugging a stack of well-constructed fabric shopping bags—handed me one in pretty shades of blue and purple. "Here you go. In exchange for your promise to forgo plastic."

The woman went on to explain she volunteered with a group that made and distributed these reusable bags at venues and events in the area. They hoped to spread awareness about the effects of plastic bags on our oceans and environment.

On a drizzly Saturday morning, I stopped by another farm stand. After sidestepping dogs and puddles, I paid for my corn, green peppers, and red onions and tucked them into my new fabric bag.

"Do you know about our CSA?" the vendor asked me.

That day, Day 298, I learned a CSA is a community-supported agriculture program. Consumers purchase a farm share and receive a biweekly treasure trove of fruits and vegetables. With varying parameters, a CSA supports local farmers and allows recipients to eat ripe, in-season produce.

So I signed up.

Every two weeks, at the pickup point, I excitedly waited to see what the farmworkers would load into my car. They'd place a bag or two brimming with kale and potatoes and green onions. Always a cantaloupe or watermelon.

As I unloaded my haul onto the kitchen counter, I contemplated how to incorporate those botanical treasures into upcoming meals. How do I cut and cook beets (Day 312)? I didn't think I liked eggplant—and had never purchased it—*but hey, I'll figure out something to do with it* (Grilled Eggplant Pasta—Day 351).

Like remodeling or re-collecting *stuff,* one new thing led to another new thing. The domino effect was sprinkled throughout this Next New Thing project. Exploring produce stands evolved into carrying (and collecting!) fabric bags that guided me to research ways to up my sustainability game. The farm stands led to discovering CSAs and giving one a whirl for a season. And that venture led to experimenting with foods and recipes and dinners.

But this domino effect was a good thing, unlike me stuffing my cabinets and drawers because I had the space. Evidence, once again, that when I jumped in and did *something*, a whole bunch of other *somethings* might go right. I didn't know where one tiny new thing could lead. It wasn't difficult or scary or mind-altering to stop by farm stands or buy kale or prepare roasted beets. But I had to decide to do it. And you know what? It felt good.

STOP! LOOK! PAY ATTENTION!

"What are you going to do?" I asked.
"Something different," she said. "There is more to
life than just continuing to do what we know."
-REBECCA SERLE, ONE ITALIAN SUMMER

On Day 43, I tugged on my pajamas, eager to settle in bed with my novel. As I turned on the lamp, I noticed the red leather notebook lying on the nightstand. The notebook where, each evening, I documented my new things.

It had been one of those days. A plumber worked most of the morning on a bathroom sink that didn't want to drain. I rushed to a dental appointment, only to learn the dentist was running 30 minutes late. An incorrectly posted check led to a phone call, then another phone call, and then an unexpected trip to the bank.

It was 9:30 p.m., and I had forgotten to do something new.

As I washed and dried my face, I agonized. I didn't want to break my new thing streak, but I was exhausted and didn't have the strength to launch my creative spirit. I dabbed on eye cream and massaged lotion into my neck. And thought. And came up with no ideas. No ideas for the day's new thing when I was ready for bed, could barely keep my eyes open, and all I wanted was to crawl under the covers and open my book.

Nothing—I had nothing.

And then, as I grabbed my toothbrush and toothpaste, the light bulb went off. I'd brush my teeth with my left hand.

Pressing the toothpaste tube, I guided the paste onto the brush's bristles. My toothbrush traveled over my teeth—up and down, back and forth—with clumsy, uncooperative strokes. Toothpaste dribbled from my mouth and trickled down the front of my pajamas. After brushing my teeth approximately 41,610 times with my right hand, the task was harder than I anticipated with my left.

I had to concentrate. While brushing my teeth with deliberate, focused strokes, my mind didn't drift to tomorrow's to-do list, the text message I wanted to send to my son before I fell asleep, or the eggs I forgot to buy at the market.

When I did that next new thing, I paid attention.

✣ ✣ ✣

We've all done it. We pile our grocery bags in the car, throw the vehicle into reverse, and back out of a parking space. As we make our way home, we ponder how we will throw together dinner, change our clothes, slap on some makeup, and head back out of the house for a 7:00 meeting at church. We pull into our garage or parking space, and that's when we realize *we don't remember how we got home.*

Oh, we understand that we *drove* home. We sat at red lights and pressed the gas pedal when those lights turned green. We waited for the intersections to clear before we made left-hand turns. We wound through our neighborhoods, navigated the familiar streets, and pulled into our driveways.

But we didn't pay attention.

Although not always as dangerous as mindlessly steering my way through traffic, it's not hard for me to shift into autopilot mode and not think about what I'm doing. Because I can't turn off my worries about the world's affairs, I read the same pages of a book over and over. Like a robot, I often stand at the kitchen counter, holding a sand-wich and my phone, forgetting I'm eating lunch. I'm sometimes guilty of *hearing*, but not *listening* to, my husband.

Call it mindfulness, call it intentionality, call it being present. When I did all those new things—whether cutting a pineapple, attempting a yoga pose, casting on knitting stitches, or making a YouTube video—I had to concentrate. I had to set aside my phone, turn off the TV, and give the cookies I decorated or the apron I stitched or the unexplored walking trail my complete attention.

Undertaking any of my new things forced me to slow down, focus, and take notice. And this consciousness carried over into familiar set-tings too.

As many times as I'd driven down Nashville's Belmont Boulevard, not once had I gone into the old-timey neighborhood market. I whooshed by it, day after day, my mind not registering that this tiny market may be the perfect place to stop for a quart of milk or the bittersweet chocolate I needed for a baking project. I had regular grocery stores, and this little gem hid from my consciousness—like a pebble-sized crack in the window or the stack of mail in the kitchen. I saw it, but I didn't notice it.

One weekday evening, I picked up dinner at a local barbecue joint—Day 318's new thing. As I crept through the rush-hour traffic, pausing at crosswalks filled with students finishing classes for the day, I spied—and smelled the smoky aroma of—the barbecue eatery. With other cars pulling in and out, I carefully maneuvered my way through the parking lot and found a space alongside another building. And that building, right next door to the barbecue spot, was *the old-timey market.*

I took a long, careful look at the lettering and signs covering the window. The signs I'd "seen" dozens of times I'd driven past, indicating the grocery sells stamps, lottery tickets, deli sandwiches, and potato salad. "We take coupons!" a hand-painted sign proclaimed, alongside a list of canned goods and ice cream on sale that week.

I was paying attention.

Before I picked up our dinner order, I popped inside the market. *How is it possible I hadn't noticed this? Hadn't been here? Missed it for so long?*

According to a friend with a counseling and behavior analysis background, "Being alive in the moment we're actually *in* is important for mental health." It's easy to worry away as we watch grandchildren swim or pull out phones when we must wait in line. But both rob us of experiencing the joys of what we're doing. "Most of us aren't good at living in the moment," she says. "It requires constant self-awareness and vigilance to remind ourselves to *just be*."

When I remember to pay attention to only what I'm doing—and, believe me, it's a continual reminder situation—I feel like I'm not missing out on life. I'm absorbed in my world.

Day 44. After a good night's sleep—and my left-handed toothbrushing incident—I hopped in the shower. Steamy water caressed my neck and cascaded down my back and legs. I squished the creamy body wash between my fingers and slathered it onto a nubby cloth. And then, unlike approximately 22,000 previous showers, I washed my right armpit first.

During the course of this project, all I did was a new thing, then another, and then the next. And all kinds of good stuff came about. That's what happened to me. And it can happen to you too.

OOPS

The key, my dear, is to make sure you don't disappoint yourself.
-FIONA DAVIS, THE SPECTACULAR

As fun as this project was, and as much as I looked forward to each day's discovery, I had those times when I didn't want to do anything new. Either I was in a crabby mood, feeling off, or simply tired of the whole deal.

On those mornings, I poured coffee, flipped on the news, and sat at the table to organize my day. And all the familiar voices joined me.

What's the use? Why bother? I'm not making friends fast enough, and I haven't found a passion. What is this accomplishing?

But, I committed to a year—to myself and my family—and so I persevered.

To check off the task—get it *over with*—I did some simple, almost silly, things.

A dedicated viewer of the *Today* show, I switched the channel to *Good Morning America* on Day 172. On another day, I brushed my teeth while standing on one foot. I tried a new radio station or Spotify playlist and dispensed a macchiato from our building's coffee machine. One December morning—Day 90—after a friend touted its benefits, I prepared a mug of hot water with lemon slices and sipped it on my balcony.

On those days when I didn't feel great or a new thing wasn't coming easily to me or I just wasn't in the mood, I still found something. I didn't break my streak.

At last, the one-year point arrived. I did it! A whole year of new things. I congratulated myself and announced to my family that I had accomplished my goal.

And then I made a big mistake.

✛ ✛ ✛

During the year, I tried many new things I didn't like. Or they didn't work for me. Like meditation. Devotees praise the benefits of this mind-clearing practice—managing stress, focusing on the present, improving sleep quality. But it made me *nervous* to lie on the floor, eyes closed, body still, palms to the sky. On Day 160, sneaking a glance at the timer I'd set, I couldn't turn off the thoughts swirling in my mind—bake a birthday cake for my husband, change the furnace filters, send Susan a sympathy card.

Zumba wasn't my cup of tea, either. The popular exercise craze incorporates high- and low-intensity dance moves to pulsing, high-energy music. The two or three classes I tried were more like dance parties than workouts. And, therein lay my problem. My hips and shoulders don't shimmy and shake with loose and wild abandon. My body doesn't relax into those moves. My body stumbles.

There were foods I wouldn't buy (kefir, Day 251) or make (chickpea cookies, Day 322) again. Television shows, movies, articles, and podcasts where I bailed before the end. Shops I won't return to.

I emailed a few women to set up a coffee date, and they never responded to my message. Another meeting I *did* have was a bust. The friendly woman and I fumbled for conversation and never found common ground. Nothing clicked. And then there was the time when I *thought* I'd found a new friend. Drinking coffee, we compared child and travel and mother-of-the-groom notes. I've not seen her since.

The foods, recipes, and movies that didn't work were easy to get over and dismiss. The people, not so much. I had no trouble letting go of chickpea cookies, but I ruminated over why some women chose not to get together with me or didn't reach out to me again. After all, I was new in town, a nice person, and I wanted to meet people!

Although we've all read that people don't think of us nearly as much as we think they do, it's hard not to blame ourselves when others don't respond. *Why hasn't she texted me back? Why hasn't she gotten back to me with a lunch date?* As humans are apt to do, we make it about ourselves. We focus on all the negative reasons we haven't heard from an individual. *What did I do wrong? Did they not like me?*

Those feelings stung, but I pressed on.

What I realize now is the unfavorite stuff I tried turned out to be as important to me as the new things I enjoyed. Looking back, I see it was fun to experiment and learn what I like to do. And not do.

Changes define life. We are constantly changing in some way. We become older, sicker, healthier, or hard of hearing. We develop cataracts, lose or gain weight, our hair turns gray. If we stop changing, we stop growing. And one step toward something new is change.

During this project, I traveled in different directions. I explored new foods, places, people, things, and thoughts. Over time, I discovered which micro paths I wanted to follow and incorporate into my life.

We only need to find a way that works for us.

✠ ✠ ✠

On September 10, 2017, at the one-year mark, I stopped. I reached my goal and no longer did something new each day. Like a basketball team leading by 20 points at halftime, I was confident. I was all smiles and high fives, and things were going my way. At the end of the year, I had a few friends, I was content in Nashville, and I didn't have to reach and stretch to survive. I had finished my project, and I relaxed.

Oh, on some days, I did new things as a matter of course. I met friends for dinner at the latest tapas place or baked a new pumpkin bread recipe or road-tripped to a different city.

But I didn't *look* for new things. Without my self-imposed assignment, I stopped seeking hikes, routes, hobbies, and events. I fell out of the habit of doing the next new thing. My project helped me settle into my community and take a hard look at myself. Surely, I could continue exploring and discovering. Undoubtedly, this pattern of new behavior had become a habit.

But, when I examined my behavior post-project, I noticed I'd returned to autopilot mode. I walked in the same parks, visited the same farm stands, and listened to the same radio stations.

When that basketball team bounds out of the locker room after halftime, players are relaxed and giddy with a victory in their sights. Then, an opposing player steals the ball, races down the court, and dunks a layup. The pesky opponents peck their way back in the game with a basket here, a steal there, and a couple of blocked shots. Before long, the overconfident team's lead shrinks, and they must find a way to pull themselves together.

I let my guard down too.

After a month or two, I studied myself. Yes, I was getting comfortable in this new place. But I was restless. A little out of sorts and a bit bored. I felt like something was missing. Like those irksome basketball opponents, my old habits began to creep up on me. Once again, I was drowning in sameness.

I missed my new things.

Many of us have read articles suggesting theories on the number of days it takes to form a habit. Some propose 21 days, others 66, while Malcolm Gladwell—in his bestseller *Outliers*—claims it takes 10,000 hours of practice to become an expert in any skill.[22] I'd executed novel activities for 365 days—much longer than 66 days, considerably less than 10,000 hours. My practice—I learned when I stopped—had not become second nature.

Once again, I reached out to Dr. Laurel Brown. According to Dr. Brown, novelty enriched my life and helped me gain a new perspective. My project affected my disposition and thoughts in a positive manner. I felt good about myself. "However, unless we are intentional on a regular basis, it is common for us to revert back to our old track, to our former, ingrained way of thinking."[23]

And so, I kicked into gear again.

As I write this, I just celebrated my 64th birthday. Seven years after plastering my laundry room with all those new thing ideas, I still find something new to do each day. Most days, anyway.

Nowadays, I'm not as vigilant and skip a day here or there, but this exercise works for me. And so I continue. After almost 2,557 days of new things, a tiny spark still ripples through me whenever I realize I'm doing something I've never done before. This week, my birthday week, I read a book about Maria Callas—an opera diva I knew nothing about.[24] I bit into—and then devoured—the most heavenly sea salt-sprinkled chocolate chunk cookie when friends treated me to lunch at Restoration Hardware. I whipped up a chia seed pudding that was truly awful and a Greek lemon soup that was sublime.

"Yes, you must have some creativity," says Dr. Brown. But "the magic formula," she continues, "is discipline, determination, and consistency."[25]

I FOUND MY *IT*

*Man needs, for his happiness, not only the enjoyment
of this or that, but hope, and enterprise, and change.*
-BERTRAND RUSSELL, AS FOUND IN MUSICAL CHAIRS
BY AMY POEPPEL

One Friday evening, I poked around the refrigerator. As I plopped a lone garlic clove, a few mushrooms, a tired-looking red pepper, and half a jar of black olives on the kitchen counter, Mark walked in the door. We planned to kick off our weekend with dinner and a movie—at home. A pizza wizard, Mark's superpower is to take bits and pieces of leftover ingredients and whip them into a delicious end-of-the-week meal. My job is to perch on a kitchen stool, sip a glass of wine, and observe.

As is customary, he uncorked a bottle of red wine, retrieved two glasses from the cupboard, and poured. Handing a glass to me, the liquid sloshing close to the rim, he said, "Let's go sit down. I want to talk to you."

Uh-oh. What is it now? This was not the usual routine.

If he proposes a different job in another city, I will lose it. I am *not* moving again. A health scare? Are the kids okay? Did he get fired? He's leaving me? My mind raced through all the—negative, of course—possibilities.

He noticed my concerned face. "It's nothing bad," he said.

In his work voice, the calm, reasonable tone that always got the attention of our young sons, he told me that he knows I'm frustrated and can't determine what I'd like to do. He also reminded me, when I sift through potential passion projects, I only consider those contributing to our financial well-being.

"But what happens if you take income out of the equation?" he asked. "What would you love to do if you could do anything at all?"

And the answer tumbled out of my mouth.

Dan Buettner, a *National Geographic* explorer and journalist, identified the five places where people live the longest with the lowest rate of chronic disease. He coined these spots the Blue Zones.

The residents of Okinawa, Japan, Sardinia, Italy, Nicoya, Costa Rica, Ikaria, Greece, and Loma Linda, California, eat well, know how to downshift, and place a high priority on friends, family, and faith. They also have a purpose. The Okinawans deem it Ikigai and the Nicoyans define it as *plan de vida*. For both communities, it means "why I wake up in the morning."[26]

According to Mr. Buettner, "If purpose were a pill, it would be a blockbuster drug." In an interview, I heard Mr. Buettner state, "People who know their sense of purpose live about eight years longer than people who are rudderless."[27]

A passion need not be a money-making endeavor or a giant undertaking. Whether knitting baby blankets for a hospital, playing in pickleball tournaments, babysitting grandkids, road-tripping to all 50 states, or experimenting with French cooking, a purpose lights a fire under us. It motivates us to leap into our days. It keeps our minds active, and it is different for all of us.

I didn't hesitate or stammer. I didn't stumble over the words as they jumped out of my mouth. This was IT.

"I'd go around and talk to people and find out what they do and how they do it and write up their story," I said.

"Then do it," he said.

Why in the world didn't he ask me this question a long time ago and save me from all my ruminating? But, before that conversation, I wouldn't have known the answer.

My husband told me that evening that, over the past year, he'd noticed my changes—the ones I couldn't see. Oh sure, I felt less frightened and more confident, but I couldn't see the bigger picture. I was too close. I was like the novelist who cannot see an alternate way for her plot and characters to unfold. But her editor, looking with objective eyes, can.

During the course of this project, taking tiny baby steps, I put myself in uncomfortable situations. At the time, I didn't realize they were uncomfortable. I thought they were new and scary and unsettling. I learned to put up with discomfort. I got used to it.

To interrupt a pattern or a habit—fearing, ruminating, controlling—we must be willing to push into the discomfort. One way to do that is to put ourselves in situations we can't control or that aren't normal to us. And sit with that uncomfortableness. We gradually train ourselves to think through how to handle a situation instead of shifting to our automatic worrisome thoughts.

✣ ✣ ✣

Of course, the relentless naysayers rushed in with their roars of negativity and a stampede of excuses.

"I'm not a writer," I protested. "Who would read the stories? Who would agree to talk with me? I can't do that."

"Who cares if no one reads them?" my husband asked. *(Well, I sort of do.)* "Do it, and see what happens."

And so I did.

Since I'm good with lists, I made one. What would I like to learn about? I jotted down everything that popped into my mind while I vacuumed the rug or unloaded the dishwasher or folded towels. *What do giraffes eat at the zoo? What's it like to travel to Iceland? How do songwriters get their ideas? How does a recipe developer write a cookbook? What's a ketubah?* The task consumed me. From the moment my feet hit the floor in the morning, I calculated how to make this work. Where should I start?

Shortly after my epiphany, we planned to travel to San Francisco for a former California neighbor's wedding. I decided it might be interesting to talk with a fortune cookie baker and learn how to stuff the written messages inside the crispy treats. Donning my impostor hat, I phoned two bakeries, introducing myself as a "Nashville writer" and requesting a brief interview. *Ha!* That approach did not work.

On my third call, Kevin answered the phone at his family's fortune cookie bakery.

"Sure, come on in," he said. He had no clue I was a nobody.

For the days leading up to my trip, I researched interviewing techniques and read as much as possible about fortune cookies. I prepared a list of questions for Kevin. I practiced recording conversations on my phone so I didn't have to take notes or rely on my memory for details.

On the big day, I set out from our hotel. Following my instructions, I turned down a deserted alley, made even gloomier by the heavy rain and gray January morning. Amid the back door entrances, fire escapes, garbage dumpsters, and signs written in Chinese characters, I spotted one tiny English sign and smiled. I was in the right place.

During the next hour, I snapped photos while Kevin demonstrated how a spigot squirts batter into tiny pancake-shaped molds on a hot rotating griddle. Two women—"family friends and employees," said Kevin—grabbed the flat cookies off the griddle, tucked a fortune in the center, and folded the cookie over rods to create the familiar fortune cookie shape. All done in four seconds before the cookie cools and hardens. He then introduced his mother, who was busy at the rear of the bakery mixing vats of batter, and his uncle, who was boxing shipments to stores and restaurants. I thanked Kevin for his time and information, as he loaded me down with bags of fortune cookies—chocolate, strawberry, and original—and heaps of encouragement.

Like Winnie the Pooh's pal, Tigger, I bounced my ebullient self back to the hotel. Bubbling over with accomplishment and happiness *(I did it!)*, I passed out cookies to the housekeepers and the parking attendants and the desk clerks.

"My kids will love these," more than one staff member said. And I gave them more.

On our plane ride home, staring out the window at the puffy clouds and munching my itty-bitty pack of pretzels, reality hit me. I had to write a story. I'd promised Kevin I'd send it to him once it was "published." So that's what I had to do. Yikes.

For the next three weeks, after I sprang out of bed, jumped into my sweats, and brushed my teeth, I plopped down at the kitchen table with my laptop and coffee. And did the next new thing. My younger son—and technology mentor—walked me through securing and registering my site's name. I wrote, tightened, and revised. I uploaded my unprofessional bakery photos and the finished story to a blogging site I had to figure out how to use and manage.

I hit PUBLISH. There it was. There I was. For all the world to see.

As I guessed, finding other people willing to talk with a woman who offered an unpolished website with one story on it, no online presence, and a meager social media following proved challenging. Who could blame the zookeeper or the songwriter or the travel writer for saying no?

Rather than throwing in the towel, I leaned into the uncomfortableness. Instead of automatically giving in to doubt, defeat, and hesitation, I attacked the next right thing one tiny step at a time. Or in my case, the next new thing.

To gain momentum and credibility, I requested interviews with people I had connections with. People who trusted me and knew I'd do a good job with the information they gave me. I interviewed a costume designer I'd met in a sewing class. The woman at the farmer's market who handed out fabric bags to folks promising to forgo plastic. A cookbook author who was the friend of a friend's daughter.

It took some time for the stories to come together—and a lot more research and learning—but more and more people I contacted began to say yes.

Without my new thing project, would the blog and podcast exist? I bet not. If I hadn't been uncomfortable in my new place and ventured out on solo field trips and ridden shotgun in a police car and dipped my toe into all those new thing waters, I doubt I would have been brave enough to tackle interviews and writing. If I had to guess, those nagging voices—fearing I will fail, people will scoff, I'm not good enough, I'm too old, it's too late, I can't do it well, why waste my time—would have stopped me in my tracks.

After I'd published four or five stories, I looked at my husband across my laptop one night.

"I'd really like this to be a success," I said.

His reply? "It already is." And he was right.

Journal of New Things

Use this space to keep track of your own new things …

---------------------------------------   ---------------------------------------

---------------------------------------   ---------------------------------------

---------------------------------------   ---------------------------------------

---------------------------------------   ---------------------------------------

---------------------------------------   ---------------------------------------

---------------------------------------   ---------------------------------------

---------------------------------------   ---------------------------------------

---------------------------------------   ---------------------------------------

---------------------------------------   ---------------------------------------

---------------------------------------   ---------------------------------------

---------------------------------------   ---------------------------------------

_____   _____

_____   _____

_____   _____

_____   _____

_____   _____

_____   _____

_____   _____

_____   _____

_____   _____

_____   _____

_____   _____

_____   _____

_____   _____

_____   _____

_____   _____

_____   _____

_____   _____

_____   _____

_____   _____

_____   _____

_____   _____

_____   _____

_____   _____

_____   _____

_____   _____

_____   _____

_____   _____

_____   _____

_____   _____

_____   _____

_____   _____

_____   _____

_____   _____

_____   _____

_____   _____

_____   _____

_____   _____

_____   _____

ABOUT THE AUTHOR

Pamela Lamp is a writer, blogger, and podcast host. On her *Who I Met Today* blog and *Who I Met Today* podcast, she interviews people from all walks of life, with topics ranging from health and food to books, aging, and travel. Her desire is to encourage listeners and readers to explore uncharted territory and learn something new every day. Pamela enjoys traveling, cooking, playing golf and pickleball, reading, and spending time with family and friends. She lives in Nashville, Tennessee, with her husband.

ENDNOTES

Finding My IT

1 Courtney Connley, "Michelle O'Bama shares the No. 1 Lesson She Learned From Her Mom," CNBC.com, May 13, 2018, https://www.cnbc.com/2018/05/11/michelle-obama-shares-the-no-1-lesson-she-learned-from-her-mom.html.

2 Aliya Alimujiang, MPH; Ashley Wiensch, MPH; Jonathan Boss, MS; et al. "Association Between Life Purpose and Mortality Among US Adults Older Than 50," jamanetwork.com, May 24, 2019, https://jamanetwork.com/journals/jamanetworkopen/fullarticle/2734064.

3 Bob Goff, *Dream Big: Know What You Want, Why You Want It, and What You're Going to Do About It* (Nashville: Thomas Nelson, 2020), title page.

Do the Next New Thing

4 Julia Cameron, *Finding Water: The Art of Perseverance* (New York: TarcherPerigee, 2009), 49.

5 Gretchen Rubin, *The Four Tendencies* (New York: Harmony, 2017), 27-29.

Go It Alone

6 Julia Cameron, *The Artist's Way Workbook* (New York: TarcherPerigee, 2006), 11.

7 Dr. R. J. Jacobs, conversation with the author, April 9, 2020.

Baby Steps

8 Dr. Laurel Brown, conversation with the author, June 29, 2021.

Prepare for Surprises

9 Tania Luna and Leeann Renninger, PhD, *Surprise: Embrace the Unpredictable and Engineer the Unexpected* (New York: Perigee, 2015), 82.

Play is for Grown-Ups

10 Sarah Steimer, "Mihaly Csikszentmihalyi, pioneering psychologist and 'father of flow,' 1934–2021," news.uchicago. edu, October 28, 2021, https://news.uchicago.edu/story/mihaly-csikszentmihalyi-pioneering-psychologist-and-father-flow-1934-2021.

Pull Out Your Phone

11 Kristi Hedges, "Stop. Reflect. Try New Things," forbes.com, October 14, 2014, https://www.forbes.com/sites/work-in-progress/2014/10/14/the-power-of-pause/?sh=153156a77368.

Let's Eat

12 Kelly Lambert PhD, *Lifting Depression: A Neuroscientist's Hands-On Approach to Activating Your Brain's Healing Power* (New York: Basic Books, 2010), 32.

13 Ibid, 45.

Trust the Odds

14 Jenn Senrich, "Boo! 6 Reasons Getting Scared is Shockingly Good for Your Health," thehealthy.com, February 25, 2021, https://www.thehealthy.com/mental-health/getting-scared-benefits/.

Keep on Worrying

15 Jenny Taitz, "How to Worry More Mindfully," nytimes.com, November 2, 2020, https://www.nytimes.com/2020/11/02/smarter-living/how-to-worry-mindfully.html.

Dating My Spouse

16 Dr. R. J. Jacobs, conversation with the author, April 9, 2020.

I Need Friends

17 Kendra Cherry MSEd, "Maslow's Hierarchy of Needs," verywellmind.com, August 14, 2022, https://www.verywellmind.com/what-is-maslows-hierarchy-of-needs-4136760.

18 Mary West and Karin Gepp PsyD, "Maslow's Hierarchy of Needs Pyramid: Uses and Criticisms," medicalnewstoday.com, July 29, 2022, https://www.medicalnewstoday.com/articles/maslows-hierarchy-of-needs.

19 Kendra Cherry MSEd, "What is the Negativity Bias?" verywellmind.com, November 14, 2022, https://www.verywellmind.com/negative-bias-4589618.

Praying Together

20 Squire Rushnell and Louise DuArt, *Couples Who Pray: The Most Intimate Act Between a Man and a Woman* (Nashville: Thomas Nelson, 2011).

21 Jamie Friedlander, "The Power of Learning New Things Together," success.com, August 14, 2019, https://www.success.com/the-power-of-learning-new-things-together/.

OOPS

22 Malcolm Gladwell, *Outliers: The Story of Success* (New York: Back Bay Books, 2011), 40.

23 Dr. Laurel Brown, conversation with the author, June 29, 2021.

24 Gill Paul, *Jackie and Maria* (New York: William Morrow, 2020).

25 Dr. Laurel Brown, conversation with the author, June 29, 2021.

I Found My IT

26 Blue Zones website, "Huge Study Confirms Purpose and Meaning Add Years to Life," bluezones.com, https://www.bluezones.com/2019/05/news-huge-study-confirms-purpose-and-meaning-add-years-to-life/.

27 The mindbodygreen Podcast, "The daily habits of people who live longer with Blue Zones founder Dan Buettner," Episode 157, 12/3/2019. https://podcasts.apple.com/us/podcast/the-mindbodygreen-podcast/id1246494475?i=1000458501937.